A FUTURE FOR
ISRAEL?

A FUTURE FOR ISRAEL?

Christian Arabs Share Their Stories

Julia Fisher

Authentic

12 11 10 09 08 07 06   7 6 5 4 3 2 1

First published 2006 by Authentic Media,
9 Holdom Avenue, Bletchley, Milton Keynes, Bucks,
MK1 1QR, UK and
129 Mobilization Drive, Waynesboro, GA 30830–4575, USA.
Authentic Media is a division of Send The Light Ltd.
(registered charity no. 270162)

British Library Cataloguing in Publication Data
A catalogue record for this book is available from the British
Library
ISBN 1-86024-531-5

Cover design by fourninezero design.
Print Management by Adare Carwin
Printed in Great Britain by J.H. Haynes Ltd., Sparkford

CONTENTS

Foreword   7

Introduction   11

Chapter One   Tom Hess   13

Chapter Two   Joseph Haddad   27

Chapter Three   George Kazoura   47

Chapter Four   Labib Madanat   57

Chapter Five   Yousef Dakwar   67

Chapter Six   Emil Boutros Boktor   81

Chapter Seven   Naim Khoury   89

Chapter Eight   Shmuel Aweida   105

FOREWORD

Do you believe in miracles? You will after you read this book. A miracle is something that is supernatural – a word which in Latin means 'above nature'. That means it is not natural. Not unnatural, but above, or beyond, what is natural: it is what defies a natural explanation.

What is described in this gripping book is one example after another of how God overruled and people did that which is right *against nature*. The most natural thing in the world is hatred. We do not need an Oxbridge education to learn to hate. It is what we naturally do when people have hurt us. But when we love and forgive those who have hurt us, we cross over into the supernatural, an arena not many explore.

Unless you have been to Israel and have talked to Israelis and Palestinians, it may be difficult to grasp just how deep the hatred is that they feel towards each other. We read about such hostility in the newspapers and some of us glibly say: 'Why don't they just decide to get along with each other?' If only it were that easy! When you get to know both Jews and Arabs you often tend to be influenced by the last person you talk to. When you are with

Jews you understand how they feel – and you want to have 'a word' with Palestinians! But when you talk with Palestinians and hear their plight, you quickly understand their feelings.

I will never forget the awakening I had when I first realised how hard it is for Palestinians who receive Jesus Christ as their Lord and Saviour to begin to read the Old Testament. They are instructed to read the Bible in order to grow in grace. But it is not long before they realise they are reading about Israelites (their ancient enemy) and Philistines (their forebears) and are told they are to submit to the God of the Bible who has chosen Israel as his covenant people. This is a giant step for them to take. To accept the Old Testament as God's very word and then not only to pray to him, but also affirm the very people he has chosen, is a journey for Palestinians that most of us cannot identify with.

It is the sheer grace of God that lies behind the accounts Julia Fisher writes about here. Only God himself could cause an Arab Christian to baptise two Jews in the River Jordan. You will read about such in this book. Tears will fill your eyes as you read about the love Palestinian Christians and Messianic Jews have for each other. This book should be read by every Christian in the world.

I have known Julia for many years. What amazes me most about her is the depth of her passion for the land of Israel, and how that is matched by a love for Israelis and Palestinians that I have not seen in many people. She longs to see reconciliation in the Middle East and carries in her heart a passion for the people in that part of the world that is exceedingly rare.

The apostle Paul talked about the 'dividing wall of hostility' being destroyed (Eph. 2:14, NIV). Sadly, we have not seen as many examples of this as we wish, but *A Future for Israel?* shows that more of this is happening than most people realise. I myself hold to the view that the blindness that is on Israel will one day be lifted (see Rom.11:25). I have wondered many times what might bring this about. But a book like this one could be used of God to precipitate this turnaround. Pray that it will have a wide distribution all over the world, especially in the Middle East. You will be absolutely convinced that *A Future for Israel?* will be a significant step in bringing Arabs and Jews together.

R.T. Kendall
Key Largo, Florida
1 November 2005

INTRODUCTION

Arabs who cherish Israel and the Jewish people? How can this be? Read on and let me introduce you to some people who may surprise you.

To introduce is to make someone acquainted with another person . . . and, quite simply, that's the purpose of this collection of true stories.

This book is addressed to the western believer who is interested in the Middle East, and what God is doing there, and who wonders how peace can ever come to Israel when she is surrounded by so many hostile Arab nations dedicated to her destruction.

Now let me turn to the people I would like you to meet. They are a small group of Arab believers; most of them are pastors. They all live in the Middle East; some in Israel, others in the West Bank, others in countries neighbouring Israel. While most have every reason to hate the Jewish people and the nation of Israel, not only have they forgiven everything in their past (and you will have to read their individual stories to realise how deep this forgiveness is), but through their study of the Scriptures, they have come to understand the strategic spiritual importance of Israel

and the Jewish people in God's plan. Their stories describe
their individual struggles. That they are prepared to share
at this sensitive and dangerous time is because they are so
keen that believers in the west hear about what is happening – how God is working, mysteriously, to unite his people, Jew and Gentile.

Julia Fisher
October 2005

Chapter One

Tom Hess

Founder of the Jerusalem House of Prayer for all Nations . . . 'the church needs to understand what God is doing in the world today and start to work with him rather than against him.'

This book aims to reveal the mystery of how God is bringing peace to the Middle East and, as you might expect, it has nothing to do with politics.

In my previous book, Israel: the Mystery of Peace *(published by Authentic Lifestyle, 2004), I described several stories of reconciliation between Jews, Arabs and Christians within Israel, the West Bank and Gaza that demonstrated how through a common belief in the purpose and power of the death and resurrection of Messiah Jesus, the 'dividing wall of hostility' that Paul mentions in his letter to Ephesians, was quite literally being 'abolished'.*

This book develops these stories of reconciliation further because something else is happening in the Middle East today that few would have thought possible a few years ago. These stories are about a number of Arab Christians; their numbers are not great but the influence these men are having is enough to show that potentially these people hold the key to peace in the Middle East. And their secret? Their understanding of God's purposes for Israel. They are brave. It takes courage to stand by your beliefs when you're accused of being a collaborator and threatened with your life.

One of the people involved in this delicate work is Tom Hess. Tom is originally from the United States, and moved to Israel in 1987 where he lives on the Mount of Olives. His house overlooks the Old City of Jerusalem, and the view from his veranda looks down onto the Golden Gate in the eastern wall and the Golden Dome on the Temple Mount – daily reminders to Tom of what this struggle is all about.

It's important to tell Tom's story first because he has been a catalyst in this process of bringing Arab and Jewish pastors together and he understands the importance of prayer and daily invests hours of his time in interceding for these people.

So let's begin by hearing how Tom came to live in Israel.

I was living in Washington DC on Capitol Hill leading a community of Christians who maintained a 24-hour watch praying for the Supreme Court, for the capital and for the government of the United States. As more people heard about what we were doing and came to join us, we were able to develop a prayer network through various churches in the city. During this time I had a vision of the United States being shaken which led to me writing a book called, *Let My People Go!* (published by Progressive Vision International). It was about the Jewish *aliyah* – the great movement of Jewish people returning to their land from the nations where they were living. I began writing the book in the US and finished it on a visit to Israel. That trip was to change the whole course of my life because one day, as I was walking across the Mount of Olives, a young Arab boy approached me and asked if he could show me a house nearby that was available to rent. Six weeks later I moved in and have lived there ever since – that was in 1987. And that's the short version of the story!

It was around 1980 that my attention was first drawn towards Israel. Until that point I had not given it much thought as I was so caught up in what I was doing. But one day, whilst living in Washington DC, I was listening to a pastor sharing from Isaiah chapter 19 and I quickly realised that this was a prophecy, which had never been fulfilled. As I listened, I really resonated with this scripture:

> In that day there will be a highway from Egypt to Assyria. The Assyrians will go to Egypt and the Egyptians to Assyria. The Egyptians and Assyrians will worship together. In that day Israel will be the third, along with Egypt and Assyria, a blessing on the earth. The LORD Almighty will bless them, saying, 'Blessed be Egypt my people, Assyria my handiwork, and Israel my inheritance.'
>
> (Isaiah 19:23–25, NIV)

In 1982 I visited Israel and during that trip God revealed his purposes for Israel and 'delivered' me from Replacement Theology. In the same week God called me to move to Israel. Needing to get the timing right, I spent a month in Jerusalem in prayer and fasting in 1984. It was then that God showed me to start the Jerusalem House of Prayer for All Nations – JHOPFAN for short. The work that is going on here today is the result of that time. But still I was not sure when God intended for me to leave America.

In 1987, as I've already mentioned, I had the vision of the US being 'shaken'. At the same time I began writing *Let My People Go!*, which I completed in Israel which is when I met the Arab boy who invited me to rent the house where I live. I waited for five years, living with that vision, but it was God's timing that I had to wait for.

It was after I arrived on the Mount of Olives, which is an Arab community interspersed with a few international Christian enclaves, that the ministry really took shape. Whilst I was living in America, my interest regarding Israel was geared towards *aliyah* and the salvation of the Jewish people. However, when I arrived here I found that the Lord had put me in the middle of an Arab community, which surprised me because I thought I'd be in western Jerusalem, where Jews live! But the Lord had clearly called me here and so I found myself renting a house overlooking both the Golden Dome on the Temple Mount and the Golden Gate. Before long I was joined by others and gradually our community formed. JHOPFAN became a reality. Six months later a Jewish person came to me and said he felt we should use his house too; and thus it happened that through an Arab and a Jew we found the houses that have been our centre for the past 18 years on the Mount of Olives.

Living in the middle of an Arab community, which is mostly Muslim, it wasn't long before God gave me a real love for the Arab people and in many ways this is the most friendly community I've ever lived in. The people are so open and hospitable. God encouraged us to reach out to our Muslim neighbours and as a result many of them have been touched by the Lord. Every year we have a big

Christmas party to which 120 Muslim children come and sing happy birthday to Jesus, hear the gospel message, and witness the love of Messiah in our community!

Very quickly, one thing led to another as we understood what God was calling us to do. He encouraged us to make contact with the Jewish and Arab leaders in Jerusalem, then in the rest of Israel and then in the Middle East and facilitate them coming together to be reconciled to each other and to worship God together. We've been involved in that process since 1990.

I was not alone here for long. The community grew quite quickly and we reached about twenty-four people, and for 18 years we stayed that size. But at the beginning of 2005, a strange thing happened – our numbers grew very fast and we became a community of 42! Currently there are five Jews and five Arabs working here – and others have joined us from around the world. Because Jews and Arabs live and work with us, our involvement in Jewish and Arab reconciliation is very intimate with issues affecting every element of our community life.

From the very beginning we organised ourselves into teams to maintain a 24-hour prayer vigil – committing at least one person to prayer at all times. Since we increased in the number of people, we have been able to maintain a corporate 24-hour prayer and worship vigil. Today our community members are praying and worshipping more than ever; our individual work within the community, although important and demanding, has become secondary to our prayer life.

You might be wondering why prayer is such an important aspect of our lives. Well, the first scripture the Lord gave when we arrived was from Isaiah chapter 62:

> I have posted watchmen on your walls, O Jerusalem; they
> will never be silent day or night. You who call on the
> LORD, give yourselves no rest, and give him no rest till he
> establishes Jerusalem and makes her the praise of the
> earth.
>
> (Isaiah 62:6,7, NIV)

So our first priority from day one has been maintaining
continuous worship and intercession here on the Mount of
Olives and it's continued ever since. Some people might
ask whether this is an onerous task. To be honest, at the
beginning it was more difficult than now because we had
fewer people. Today, we have at least three people at a time
continually praying day and night, with some watches
having more than ten people. With a committed community full-time, it is not difficult to do. I hear churches of 5,000
say they couldn't undertake such a demanding programme, but it all depends on commitment. All our people
are committed to dedicating four hours a day to worship
and intercession. Daily worshipping the Lord while inti-
mately sitting at his feet is a common purpose, vision, and
calling that we all share.

It was as a result of the prayer and worship that we
became increasingly aware of God's heart for reconciliation and we saw his plan unfolding. We started inviting
Jewish and Arab pastors from Jerusalem to our house to
pray together. Then we went around the country and
introduced Jewish and Arab leaders to each other. This
might sound strange but we discovered that in many cities
they did not even know each other existed! Once introduced, they started meeting together to worship and pray.
We then started a national meeting once a year when

many of the leaders come together to worship God and pray together for more congregations to be started throughout Israel and for the reconciliation process to spread.

In the early days we concentrated on Jewish and Arab leaders being reconciled to one another. As this started to happen we understood that its purpose was to then work together to see others reconciled to God and to each other, so we started moving in that direction as well. Because nothing like this had happened before, we had to ask God to show us each step of the way. He taught us through the Scriptures. For example, we read in 2 Corinthians chapter 5:

> All this is from God, who reconciled us to himself through Christ and gave us the ministry of reconciliation.
>
> (2 Corinthians 5:18,19, NIV)

And in Ephesians we read:

> For he himself is our peace, who has made the two one and has destroyed the barrier, the dividing wall of hostility, by abolishing in his flesh the law with its commandments and regulations. His purpose was to create in himself one new man out of the two, thus making peace, and in this one body to reconcile both of them to God through the cross, by which he put to death their hostility.
>
> (Ephesians 2:14–16, NIV)

In the context of the Middle East, we understood clearly that the 'one new man' is Jew and Gentile, which in this case meant Arab.

Isaiah chapter 19, already mentioned above, contained some further foundational scriptures for us. The prophet talks about how Egypt, Israel and Assyria will worship God together and be 'a blessing on the earth'.

So in 1993 we held the first Middle East convocation in Egypt. When the 30 Messianic leaders from Israel and 70 Christian leaders from Egypt first met, they were scared of each other. As if that was not a big enough challenge, the Lord showed us that he not only wanted leaders from Israel and Egypt to meet, but also from the whole Middle East. So that same year we held two more meetings in Cyprus and pastors came from most of the other Arab nations surrounding Israel. It was a profound time. Since then, for many years we held at least one meeting a year, lasting four days at a time. That was until 2004 when the Lord showed us that he wanted us to meet twice a year. Since then we have a four-day meeting every year in Cyprus and another in Jordan. In May 2005 we met in Jordan where 80 leaders gathered; some came from the Gulf States; there were seven Iraqi pastors there; pastors from Lebanon; from Syria; 20 came from Jordan; 30 from Israel; quite a few from Egypt – Jews and Arabs coming together to worship the Lord. For the first time Iraqis were able to attend because of the change in political climate in Iraq.

The atmosphere at these meetings is sometimes difficult to describe. They are passionate people. In the early years it was not always easy to transcend politics because there was such a lack of understanding of the Scripture and many of the people were not flowing in the Spirit to the degree that they are today. In comparison, from 2001 until today there have been a number of real breakthroughs because people are moving more in the Holy Spirit. In addition we have taught about God's covenant with Israel and the church and consequently many of the Arabs are embracing the word of God. When they do this, they not only embrace God's covenant with Abraham in Genesis 15:6,18 in regards to righteousness but also in regard to the land. By embracing the covenant that God has made as well as embracing the importance of Jews and Arabs being reconciled in the Messiah, we have found a growing unity developing among the leaders from all over the Middle East as we come together. And as a result, we worship the Lord in spirit and in truth. There are no words to describe the wonder of this. Only God can bring such harmony and oneness of mind and spirit.

We do find that for some, unity is based in trying to bring opposite poles together through mutual compromise. We have experienced that this sort of unity is superficial and soon breaks down under pressure. However, if unity is based upon the whole counsel of God, by worshipping the Lord in spirit and in truth, and by embracing the word of God and God's covenants, then we find the unity is much stronger. That unity overcomes every political, social, and economic pressure. In other words, nothing is certain unless it is based upon the person of God – Father, Son, and Holy Spirit – and his word.

When an Arab pastor grasps God's revelation in the way I have described, it can be a very challenging thing for him to go back to his own country and his own people and explain it to them. However, we have found time and time again, that when people really have revelation from the Lord they become bold. Many of these Arab pastors are not only teaching the truth of God's word to the people in their own church but, in addition, to many of the pastors and leaders in their country. Obviously it varies from country to country. Some of them are teaching just a few people in their congregation depending on what situation they are in. But many of them are moving forward in teaching others and helping them to understand God's covenants with both righteousness and the land, and encouraging them into reconciliation between Jew and Arab through Jesus the Messiah. So it's slowly, slowly beginning to spread. I now see strong men of God, real pillars which God has raised up, in most of the Arab nations. These men are leading the way. They are like the first-fruit of the harvest and encourage us to keep working until we see the reality of the vision of Isaiah chapter 19 being completely fulfilled in God's perfect time.

So much has happened in the past few years, especially in recent months, so it is obvious these signs are of gathering momentum. In addition to the two convocations we hold each year for the pastors, we organise a Jewish/Arab leadership 'family camp' in the summer for those living in Israel. And now, during Rosh Hashanah and Yom Kippur between 400 and 500 Jews and Arabs come together to celebrate these holidays. People are keen to come. I think we are all realising that where politics has failed, God is showing that he has a better plan. It's a beautiful thing to see people's hearts being changed, enabling them to come together in this way. We can see that the enemy has tried to sabotage the purposes of God in this part of the world in the biggest possible way. Therefore we know that God is going to release his biggest blessing through this region of the world.

It is my opinion that these Arab pastors hold the key to peace in the Middle East. I believe that one of the main

ways we are going to see God working to release reconciliation in the Middle East, and see Jews and Arabs worshipping God together, is through the Arab believers in
Jesus. I have said many times that whilst the Muslims have
been throwing bombs at the Jewish people, other former
Muslims who have received Jesus as their Messiah are
saying to the Jewish people, 'We love you, we bless you,
we believe in your Messiah.' To the Jews this is like a spiritual bomb! It blows their mind because they see these
people's lives have been transformed. I think it's a major
key to bringing change in the Middle East.

But there is also something serious going on that we really need to pray about. Many of the Arab pastors and
Christians, whilst they have accepted the covenant in
regard to righteousness (Genesis 15:6), many of them have
rejected the covenant with the land (Genesis 15:18).
Because of this, I believe, one of the biggest attacks against
Isaiah chapter 19 coming to pass is that over the last 50
years there has been a considerable exodus of Christians
from the Middle East. They have rejected the covenant with
the land and instead have been influenced by the covenant
of death with Islam. They perceive the Middle East as
being a Muslim region. They have said, 'We are Christians
so we are going to go to the western Christian nations.'
They feel they have lost their identity here. But if they can
find their identity not only in Jesus, but also in God's
covenant with the land, then they will find their inheritance in the land and they will stay and influence the
Middle East. When they take ownership and responsibility
for the Middle East, we will see real breakthrough and the
prophecy of Isaiah 19:23–25 being fulfilled. If that were to
happen we could see a million Arab Christians returning

from all over the world to the Middle East. Until that happens, I do not believe we will see Isaiah chapter 19 being fulfilled in a fuller way.

I believe that because God has said it will happen, we will see something start to happen in the hearts of the Arab Christians and other believers who receive Jesus. We will watch as they start to recognise that they too have an inheritance in the covenant God made with Abraham. We will see them find their identity and respond to their calling and destiny to stay in the Middle East and not go to Australia or Canada or Brazil or the United States. I believe they will come to understand their role in God's purposes as they realise that God does not say he is going to make any of those countries a blessing in the midst of the earth worshipping God together! Their destiny and calling is definitely to stay in this region and become a light to the nations – Egypt, Israel and Assyria worshipping God together. So the seriousness of this is very real and there needs to be a revelation of this to the Arab Christians. The statistics say it all – 20 years ago Jordan was 17 per cent Arab Christian, today it is 3 per cent; 15 years ago Iraq, at the time of the first Gulf war, was 10 per cent Christian, today it is 2 per cent Christian; Lebanon 20 years ago was 60 per cent Christian, now it's 30 per cent Christian; Israel 50 years ago was 40 per cent Arab Christian, now it is 3 per cent. The West Bank, biblically called Judea and Samaria, was 20 per cent Christian, now it is 1 per cent. The emigration of Arab Christians from the Middle East is because the Arab Christians in these nations have instead been persuaded that life would be better for them in the west or Australia. They are not recognising and identifying their inheritance in God's covenant with

Abraham in regard to the land nor taking ownership and responsibility and believing God for Isaiah chapter 19 to come forth. They have prioritised education and comfort more than prioritising God's covenant and believing God for his word to come to pass. They are leaving the Middle East by the millions to go to the west because they say the west is Christian. But the highest calling and destiny for them is to stay in the Middle East and be a blessing in the midst of the earth. They have bought into the covenant of death with Islam and have been leaving instead of believing they are to be the greatest blessing in the midst of the earth. Only a small minority are buying into the covenant of life that is God's covenant with Abraham in regards not only to righteousness but also to the land – land he's covenanted from the Nile to the Euphrates. I believe this matter is very important and Christians in the Middle East and worldwide should be praying to understand what God is saying.

In short, the church in the west needs a revelation of God's covenant with Israel and the Middle East if it is to really understand what God is doing in the world today and start to work with him rather than against him.

For further details about Tom Hess' books and the work of JHOPFAN, contact: Jerusalem House of Prayer for All Nations, PO Box 31393, Jerusalem 91313, Israel. Email: materials@jhopfan.org

Chapter Two

Joseph Haddad

'They call me a Lebanese with a Jewish heart!'

Today Joseph Haddad is the pastor of a Lebanese church in Nahariya, a city on the coast of northern Israel only ten minutes drive from the Lebanese border which lies to the north, and a 40-minute drive from his home in Haifa, to the south.

Haifa is a unique city in Israel because Jews and Arabs live there cheek by jowl, in mixed neighbourhoods unlike other parts of Israel or the West Bank, where communities are often segregated into clearly definable villages or districts.

Joseph's story is interesting not least because he has been in the right place at just the right time. When the Israeli Defence Forces (IDF) withdrew from southern Lebanon in 2000 and 6,000 Lebanese refugees came flooding into northern Israel, he, along with his wife, was there; it was as though his life had been but a preparation for that moment and when the Lebanese arrived, Joseph realised his destiny. It was the catalyst that caused him to respond.

Today, an average week finds him travelling three or four times back and forth from Haifa to Nahariya. He holds a worship

*meeting every Friday night; a Bible study every Monday night;
a youth meeting and Sunday school every Wednesday night.
And as well as Lebanese people, much to Joseph's surprise and
delight he now finds Jewish people attending his church. How
can this be? What or who has attracted local Jewish people to this
Arab-speaking Lebanese Christian community?*

*I arranged to meet Joseph one day in early January 2005. My
husband and I were staying in a hotel overlooking the bay in
Haifa. It was a very wet and stormy day. As we looked out of our
hotel window, high above the bay, we could see the dark storm
clouds blowing in from the Mediterranean. It was raining so
hard the roads resembled gushing streams; water was pouring
down the steep flights of steps that lead down the hillside to the
old part of the city. It was not a good day for travelling. But
Joseph was undeterred and arrived on time, complete with his
black umbrella and raincoat – it reminded me of a wet winter's
day in London when people hurry about with their black umbrellas up, pushing against the strong winds that whistle around the
corners of the tall buildings, catching people unaware and turning umbrellas inside out!*

*Joseph is a tall man with deep brown compassionate eyes that
betray the fact he's seen a bit of life. He has a calm, unhurried
disposition, and a warm, friendly manner; he greeted us like long
lost friends . . . he seemed genuinely pleased to meet us.*

*'Oh the journey was fine . . . just took a little longer than
usual.' He shrugged it off and we sat down in the hotel foyer
with mugs of hot tea and he started to tell his story.*

'I was born in Haifa in 1958; I am the youngest of three
boys; my parents came from Lebanon and so I am a
Lebanese born in Israel! They call me a Lebanese with a
Jewish heart!'

I was a little surprised; he seemed to be showing a very positive attitude early on in the interview! Surely it hadn't been as easy as that?

'Some years before the State of Israel was established in 1948, my parents moved from Lebanon to live in Haifa, in northern Israel. In 1948 they decided to stay in their house even though many other Arab families fled to different countries in the Middle East. My father worked as a baker in Haifa. He was employed by a Jewish man who was very kind and encouraged him to stay and promised that he would protect us. Looking back on the events of those days, which were very uncertain, I can clearly see that this was God's plan for our family and I understand now just how much God's favour was on us.

'I went to school in Haifa. It was a Catholic school; a very strict Catholic school.' He paused. 'It was very disciplined – that's why my English is so good!

'I had some Jewish friends because Haifa is a mixture of Jews and Arabs, it always has been; it's the best model for co-existence in Israel and as a result, it's much easier and quite natural to get to know people from "the other side". But I must be honest and tell you that before I became a Christian I did not love Jews.

'During my early teens I became a very troubled and difficult person to live with. I was born when my father was sixty, and being the youngest child in the family my parents spoiled me. By the time I was a teenager my two older brothers had married and I was left at home with my parents and by this time they were quite elderly. I used to mistreat them and curse them, and throw things at them . . . it was a kind of rebellion. I didn't want to behave like that but I couldn't help it . . . it was as though something was forcing me to behave in this way. Rather than grow out of this pattern of behaviour I got worse, and it continued for several years. I was in a dilemma and deep down felt very ashamed of myself.

'I remember once waking up in the middle of the night to go to the bathroom. As I walked past my parents' bedroom I heard a voice. I stopped to listen and realised it was my mother praying. "Lord, change him," she said, "change him." She was sitting up in her bed pleading with God to change me!

'Now we were just a nominal Catholic family. We weren't into church-going or praying in a big way! We went to church – sometimes. But here was my mother sitting up in her bed in the middle of the night praying for me to be changed. I stood rooted to the spot and as I listened to her anguished voice I felt so ashamed of myself because whilst I was mistreating her, she was praying for me.

'But I didn't change. In fact my behaviour got worse as I grew older.

'Two or three years later in 1983, when I was twenty-five years of age, my parents arranged my marriage; they brought me a wife from Lebanon! They thought that maybe if I got married my violent, unpleasant behaviour would change. But the result was the complete opposite. Whilst in the past I'd had two people to mistreat, now I had three; my father, my mother and now my wife.

'When we first met, she made it clear she didn't want to marry me! But for some reason she finally agreed and we were married in the summer of 1983. For the next six months, from August 1983 until February 1984, I drove my wife crazy. I swore at her; I abused her, and twice she packed her bags and wanted to go back to Lebanon. She said, "You brought me to a crazy man; I can't live with such a man."

'But in February 1984 we went to visit some relatives and whilst at their home we met three people from the Baptist church in Haifa. For the first time in my life I heard the story of salvation. Remember, I was a nominal Christian, a Catholic. I used to go to the Catholic church maybe twice a year, at Christmas and at Easter, not to pray, just to meet friends and pass the time of day.

'But when those three brothers started talking about salvation, and forgiveness of sins and starting a new life with Jesus, I started crying. This was what I needed to hear. For 12 years I had not shed one tear; I had a stony, hard heart. If you abuse your parents and mistreat them, you've got to have a stony heart. But that night in February 1984, the Holy Spirit convicted me that I was a sinner but now I had an opportunity to be changed.

'So there I was, twenty-five years old, unhappily married and working in land surveying. My mind was in turmoil. I could not control my emotions. I was being faced with the awfulness of my own character and I didn't like what I saw and I wanted to change and be rid of this bad behaviour.

'One of the three brothers noticed I was under conviction. He pointed to me and said, "Would you like to pray?" I was astonished and said, "I don't know how to pray. I only know how to speak bad words and how to curse." He said, "Whatever's on your heart, pray it." And believe me, I prayed the sinner's prayer of repentance without anybody leading me. "Jesus, I'm a sinner. I deserve death. Please forgive me. By your grace I want to start a new life."

'I don't know where the words came from, but immediately I felt as though a burden had been removed from my back and I knew, I was convinced, that Jesus was listening to me. Suddenly, everything was shining and filled with light; everything had changed! The first thing I did was hug my wife! I was crying and asking her forgiveness. Then I went to my parent's home and took a basin of water and I washed my mother and father's feet whilst kissing them and asking their forgiveness! The change in my life was immediate and drastic! Even they did not believe I could have changed. They thought I was performing because I had been so bad. I had every bad attitude that it's possible to have and that's how people had become used to me behaving.

'When my father and mother saw the change in my life, they also received Jesus. My father was eighty-four years old when he received Jesus. Because his eyesight was so weak, he asked me to sit and read the Bible to him. Every day he said to the Lord, "Lord, why didn't you reveal yourself to me at an earlier age?"

'When our neighbours came into the house and saw me sitting and reading the Bible to my parents they said, "Praise God, a miracle has happened!" They were so used to me cursing and breaking things and attacking and mistreating them, and now they saw me coming and sitting and reading to my parents from the Bible!

'This demonstrates God's grace; I didn't deserve to be treated in this way but God not only saved me, he saved my parents and my wife when they saw the change in me! In the beginning they did not believe I had really changed. At first they were suspicious. And I'm not surprised! I had been a very bad person for a very long time, so obviously it took a little time for them to catch up with what had happened to me! It was interesting to watch the people in our neighbourhood, both Jews and Arabs, react to the change in my behaviour – it was amazing to see them coming and opening their mouths in astonishment!

'As for my wife, she did not believe me at first – she thought it was only an act. But in time she realised the change in me was genuine. And it took a little time, and I don't blame her because she was fully correct – I was so bad; she had only known me as a bad person. Now she was living with a stranger! But today we are still together, all these years later – it's amazing.

'Sometimes I look back at those days and I say, "Lord, I'm amazed that you didn't get rid of me because I was so bad. You should have thrown something from heaven and got rid of me. But you had mercy on me." I identify with the apostle Paul when he said in his first letter to Timothy chapter 1, "Christ Jesus came into the world to save sinners – of whom I am the worst." This is my story – I was exactly like that.

'And so I started devouring the Bible. I was so hungry for the word of God that I enrolled at the Assemblies of God Bible School in Haifa and studied there for three years. At the same time my wife was studying music . . . she's a worship leader now and she plays the piano. Then in 1996 I was ordained as a pastor – the call of God was on my life. It was amazing how he turned me from a wretched sinner to a minister of the gospel.

'I did not have a church at that time but the Lord was preparing me for the ministry. I was doing a lot of evangelism and I was also working with Pastor David Davis at the House of Victory rehabilitation centre in Haifa.

Actually, how that came about is very interesting. It was before I went to Bible College, David and Karen Davis had just come to live in Israel. I'd recently been saved and one night I was preaching in the Baptist Church in Haifa about repentance and holiness. That night David came to visit the church and was surprised when he heard me preaching! The Lord spoke to him immediately and told him that he should be working with me and so he took me to work with him in the House of Victory! Those early days in 1989 were so exciting. We worked hard together preparing the House of Victory; we had to clear all the weeds from the garden . . . that was before I went to Bible school.

'Then when I graduated from the Bible School, David offered me a job back at the House of Victory, and so I became one of the staff there, discipling the people in the house and teaching them the word of God. We saw many lives restored. Little did I realise it then, but I was about to be faced with my greatest challenge yet.

'In May 2000, the war in Lebanon reached a climax when the Hezbollah took over southern Lebanon and the IDF pulled out. In a matter of only a few hours, Lebanese refugees came flooding into northern Israel. Immediately, my wife and I felt a burden in our hearts to reach out to them with the Good News because these people had been forced to leave everything behind. Some of them came in their pyjamas – they did not have time to bring any of their belongings. Can you imagine how in four hours you can lose everything and enter a different land with a different language, and an uncertain future? Whilst these people were given shelter in a kibbutz in the north, David Davis called me on the phone. For some time he'd had a burden because he was anticipating that these Lebanese people would come to Israel. He also knew in his heart that because my wife is Lebanese and I have a Lebanese background that we would have a role to play in helping these people. So as we heard the news about these refugees arriving he called me and said, "Joseph, do you know where those Lebanese are staying?" I said, "Yes, I know exactly where they are because my sister-in-law has called to say she has come with them." My wife's sister is married to a Lebanese army officer and they also had to withdraw from Lebanon.

'So the next day we filled two vans with diapers and baby food, powdered milk, Arab Bibles, and we drove up to the kibbutz.

'Now this again is an amazing story. When we got there, the people were really troubled and confused and obviously feeling discouraged that the situation had got so bad so quickly. None of them knew whether or not they would be able to return home, and all had left in a hurry and quite literally fled the country. So my wife immediately set up her keyboard in the open air, and we started singing worship songs. Very soon the women and children came to listen; the men stayed away at first. But gradually some of them came and surrounded us and after we had sung several worship songs, Pastor David brought a message based on verses from Isaiah 29:

> Soon – and it will not be very long – the wilderness of Lebanon will be a fertile field once again. And the fertile fields will become a lush and fertile forest. In that day deaf people will hear words read from a book, and blind people will see through the gloom and darkness. The humble will be filled with fresh joy from the LORD. Those who are poor

will rejoice in the Holy One of Israel. Those who intimidate and harass will be gone, and all those who plot evil will be killed. Those who make the innocent guilty by their false testimony will disappear. And those who use trickery to pervert justice and tell lies to tear down the innocent will be no more.

(Isaiah 29:17–21, NLT)

'I was translating into Arabic because the people didn't speak English and they were amazed to hear that Lebanon was mentioned in the Bible and it was such a blessing for them to hear David preaching about their homeland in this way. Later one of the refugees told me (he was a Lebanese officer) that he had been going to the Catholic church in his village and he was now upset because the priest had never mentioned that Lebanon was talked about in the Bible! So when Pastor David brought this message from Isaiah 29, many of them came forward and received Jesus with tears in their eyes. At that first meeting we knew God had brought them . . . they had lost everything yet God was embracing them and loving them and showing Jesus to them as the only Saviour.

'So for the next seven months we went up to this kibbutz at least once a week to teach them the Bible and care for their physical needs. After seven months the Israeli government started to find them more permanent homes and about three hundred Lebanese families chose to come and live in Nahariya, and this is amazing because the name means River of God. It's no coincidence that God has brought them to this place called the River of God because he wants to send his river into the hearts of these people. When they moved to Nahariya, we immediately started a home group with one of the believing families and very soon, within three months we outgrew their living room! We had to move into the garden! It was summer-time so we enjoyed three months meeting outside in the open air. But this could not continue because winter was coming and we had to find another meeting place. So we cried out to God.

'And the Lord was faithful. He provided a beautiful house on the main road of the city just 100 metres from the beach promenade – a strategic place. And guess what, this home used to be the house of the first mayor of Nahariya – he had recently passed away and so we were able to rent it from his children.

'To me this was symbolic and another example of how God gives authority to the right body – to the church, because when the mayor was living there, many important decisions were taken in that property. And now God has taken the opportunity to give the authority to another group of people – to the church in Nahariya.

'The church kept growing and right now we have about one hundred adults plus children and we're outgrowing the mayor's house and now need another place – urgently!

'At the same time something amazing is happening in Nahariya in our Lebanese congregation – Jewish people are starting to come to the meetings . . . local Jews from Nahariya. And guess what, they were invited by the Lebanese to come to the meeting! I have recently baptised two Jews in the River Jordan!

'The Lord has brought the Lebanese to Nahariya to provoke the Jews who live there – can you imagine that?'

By this time Joseph's voice was breaking with emotion. It seemed that even he had been surprised at the speed at which God had been working and the comparative ease by which everything had come about. It was as though God was moving before him arranging all the details and putting everything in place; Joseph was watching something unfolding before his very eyes – things that he could never have imagined would be possible; Jewish people being drawn to a Lebanese congregation? I asked him how he coped with this . . . he used to hate Jews . . . had he experienced a change of heart?

'Let me take you back to my early days. When I grew up I told you I had a mixture of Arab and Jewish friends but because I heard the news and watched the media reports on television, I grew up with hatred towards the Jews. I was told they took the land belonging to Arabs, they mistreated the Arabs and oppressed them. And when you grow up with that sort of information being fed into you, something happens in your heart and I was definitely indifferent to Jews; I did not like them very much. However, all that started to change when I was saved in February 1984. I told you how I was devouring the Scriptures and when I read Joel 3:2, I reached a turning point in my life regarding my attitude towards Jews because I read how God will judge the nations that scattered his people Israel:

> I will gather the armies of the world into the valley of Jehoshaphat. There I will judge them for harming my people, for scattering my inheritance among the nations, and for dividing up my land.
>
> (Joel 3:2, NLT)

'Because they divided my land . . . as I read those words I realised that God says this is his land – not Jewish land or Arabic land, it's God's land and he has given it to the Jews. So when I read this verse it dawned on me – if it's God's land and he gave it to the Jews, who am I to resist him or oppose him? The word of God is so powerful, when you read it with faith it brings change into your life. So this verse was a turning point in my life. God said to me, "If I gave the Jews this land can you oppose me or resist me?" I said, "No . . . if you gave them this land, I surrender and I agree." And from that point on the Lord gave me such a love for the Jews. It may be hard for you to believe, but I pray for their salvation more than the Arabs – God has given me such a heart and I intercede for them because the Bible says, "To the Jews first."'

At this point Joseph wept and for a few minutes we paused our conversation. I wondered what many Christians in the west would think when they read this; so many take sides . . . do we really understand God's heart?

'I couldn't love them before my conversion . . . the Lord is so amazing . . . when he saved me, he changed my heart,' he said through his tears. He wept some more. 'It's such a joy for me to see Jewish people coming to my congregation. I say, "Lord, I'm not worthy – you send Jewish people to me for me to pastor, I don't deserve that."' And he wept some more.

'And how do they respond to you as an Arab/Lebanese pastor?' I asked him.

'They love me so much – they feel that my love for them is genuine, and not fake. Recently, an elderly Jewish man called Yakov asked me to baptise him; he's seventy-five years old. He was a friend of Menachem Begin. They fought side by side in the Irgun, the Jewish resistance movement. Actually he told me a story which I think will be sad for you. He was involved in blowing up a wing of the King David Hotel in Jerusalem in July 1946 and he repented in tears for that because 91 people were killed, including some British administrators who were working in the hotel and 20 British soldiers. So this is incredible to me.'

I asked Joseph if we could contact Yakov to hear his side of the story. A few days later, after returning to England, I received an email. Joseph had been to visit Yakov and wrote to tell me that two weeks after his conversion, Yakov had an amazing experience. He described how 'the enemy tried to put an end to his life'. He had a severe heart attack whilst alone in his home. The last thing he remembered before he collapsed was knocking on his neighbour's door and saying, 'Yeshua, I commit my soul into your hands.' His neighbour called an ambulance and on arrival at the Intensive Care unit of the local hospital he was pro-nounced clinically dead. The doctors tried to revive him with electric shock treatment and managed to get his heart beating again. But Yakov lay unconscious for three days. The doctors told him that when he opened his eyes on the fourth day they considered it a miracle – he had come back from the dead. Later Yakov described to Joseph what he experienced during those three days. 'He saw Yeshua dressed in a white robe surrounded by the most marvel-lous light. Yeshua held his hand and took him through heaven. He showed him the beauty of the heavenly Jerusalem where we will spend all eternity with him. As a new believer, Yakov hadn't read the book of Revelation before this experience, but the description that he shared fits exactly with the description found in Revelation chapter 21:10–27:

So he took me in spirit to a great, high mountain, and he showed me the holy city, Jerusalem, descending out of heaven from God. It was filled with the glory of God and sparkled like a precious gem, crystal clear like jasper. Its walls were broad and high, with twelve gates guarded by twelve angels. And the names of the twelve tribes of Israel were written on the gates. There were three gates on each side – east, north, south, and west. The wall of the city had twelve foundation stones, and on them were written the names of the twelve apostles of the Lamb.

The angel who talked to me held in his hand a gold measuring stick to measure the city, its gates, and its wall. When he measured it, he found it was a square, as wide as it was long. In fact, it was in the form of a cube, for its length and width and height were each 1,400 miles. Then he measured the walls and found them to be 216 feet thick (the angel used a standard human measure).

The wall was made of jasper, and the city was pure gold, as clear as glass. The wall of the city was built on foundation stones inlaid with twelve gems: the first was jasper, the second sapphire, the third agate, the fourth emerald, the fifth onyx, the sixth carnelian, the seventh chrysolite, the eighth beryl, the ninth topaz, the tenth chrysoprase, the eleventh jacinth, the twelfth amethyst.

The twelve gates were made of pearls – each gate from a single pearl! And the main street was pure gold, as clear as glass.

No temple could be seen in the city, for the Lord God Almighty and the Lamb are its temple. And the city has no need of sun or moon, for the glory of God illuminates the city, and the Lamb is its light. The nations of the earth will walk in its light, and the rulers of the world will come and bring their glory to it. Its gates never close at the end of day because there is no night. And all the nations will bring their glory and honor into the city. Nothing evil will be allowed to enter – no one who practices shameful idolatry and dishonesty – but only those whose names are written in the Lamb's Book of Life. (NLT)

In the email, Joseph described how Yakov told him of his one regret. 'What is that?' he asked him.

'That I didn't have a camera to film all the amazing beauty of the heavenly Jerusalem.'

'There is no doubt that the enemy tried to get rid of this precious brother,' continued Joseph, 'but the Lord turned all this for good. He came out of this experience with more love and steadfastness in his faith in Yeshua and is now certain that eternal life is a reality. In fact, he expressed his disappointment for coming back to this planet; he would have preferred to stay there with Yeshua.

'It is really amazing to hear Yakov telling people about this wonderful experience. God has a destiny for him. He has preserved his life and he is the first-fruit, the first Jewish believer, at our Lebanese congregation. I believe he will be the one who will bring many other local Jews to salvation through faith in Yeshua in the city of Nahariya.'

To return to Joseph's story, why does he believe so many refugees have come from southern Lebanon into Israel at this time?

'I believe they are not here by mistake. God is a God of order. The Lord spoke to me and my wife several times; he has brought them from Lebanon to a city of refuge and shelter here in Israel and he has brought them here to reveal Jesus to them; to change their lives and fill them with the Holy Spirit. In due time he will send them back to Lebanon as little sparks to start a big fire of revival all over Lebanon. You know, Lebanon now is a big mess – the government has no power. The terror organisations based in Syria are in control. But if you read Isaiah 29 it speaks about a green land. So I believe sending the Lebanese here is part of God's plan for sending revival to Lebanon. That's why me and Pastor David don't take this ministry lightly. It's something which is on God's heart. And one more thing – we are talking about the one new man – Jews and Arabs together. The Lebanese congregation is mainly Arab; David Davis's congregation is Messianic . . . here a Jewish congregation is reaching out to Arabs. And so if we are talking about the one new man, this is a good example of it – Jews reaching out to Arabs. We have many, many Arab congregations in the north, but the only congregation to have a burden for the Lebanese was a Jewish Messianic congregation. God is faithful. He gave me a love for the Jews. He gave the Jews a love for the Arabs.'

Such an unusual situation must attract attention; so, I asked Joseph how he is viewed by other Arab pastors?

'In the past, say ten years ago, the Arab pastors were, in general, reluctant to co-operate with Messianic Jews and Messianic leaders. Today there is a change in the land. I see more openness in the hearts of Arab pastors towards the Jews. There are more meetings now, more prayer meetings, more coming together. Ten years ago, only a handful of us Arab Christians were prepared to co-operate with Jewish believers. I must be honest and say not every Arab pastor feels as I do – there is a small minority who still do not want to have anything to do with Jews, but God is sifting – he wants to do a great work in Israel, and those who are willing to yield to him and co-operate with him are going to flow with this river. He's sending a river to Israel very soon – we feel that. And if you want to be a part of this river you have to love the Jews; you have to love your enemies. So God is sending a big work and I want to flow with this work, and flow with the river of the Holy Spirit, because there is a great joy and a great blessing attached to this.

'I don't mind if they talk about me or persecute me. I will give you an example – next week, Tom Hess from the House of Prayer for All Nations in Jerusalem, has organised a special event when we will spend a day going to areas where Abraham and Isaac and Jacob built altars – places like Hebron – and there we will repent (it's called identificational repentance) for what the Arabs did to the Jews and what the Jews did to the Arabs. So I am going along with another Arab pastor; we were the only ones to accept Tom's invitation. The other Arab pastors did not want to come because they are afraid of persecution. But I am not afraid; I would rather obey God than man.'

'Where does the persecution come from?' I asked Joseph.

'It comes mainly from the traditional churches – the Catholic Church and the Orthodox Church, and also some evangelical churches who believe in Replacement Theology. They accuse us of being Zionists because we love the Jews and that we co-operate with the Jews for our own selfish interests. Some people call us collaborators.'

'What would you say to the church in the west that does believe in Replacement Theology?' I asked.

'I have only one thing to say to them – they need to read Romans 9, 10 and 11 where the apostle Paul teaches how God's call and gifts to the Jews are irrevocable. To me it is a privilege to work with God in being a means to bring the Jews to salvation. If we have this privilege why should we miss it? We should flow with it and obey God because he is about to do a great work in Israel. Let me also refer to Isaiah 19 – this speaks about a highway from Egypt and Assyria, all the way to Israel.

> In that day Egypt and Assyria will be connected by a highway. The Egyptians and Assyrians will move freely between their lands, and they will worship the same God. And Israel will be their ally. The three will be together, and Israel will be a blessing to them. For the LORD Almighty will say, 'Blessed be Egypt, my people. Blessed be Assyria, the land I have made. Blessed be Israel, my special possession!'
>
> (Isaiah 19:23–25, NLT)

'God speaks about these three nations, Assyria (which incorporates modern day Syria, Iraq and Lebanon), Egypt and Israel, and states that those nations will one day be a blessing to the whole earth. At the moment we don't see those blessings! These nations are not a blessing at all . . . all the bad news comes from the Middle East! But because God's word is trustworthy, it is going to be fulfilled one day. I believe God is going to send a big revival into Israel. As the apostle Paul says, ". . . since the Jews' rejection meant that God offered salvation to the rest of the world, how much more wonderful their acceptance will be. It will be life for those who were dead!" (Romans 11:15, NLT).

'So let's be obedient to God and let him do the work, and let us be a part of this work.

'Praise God!'

Chapter Three

George Kazoura

. . . From communism to compassion

In northern Israel, in the village of Rama (well known for its olive presses) is an orphanage called the 'House of Love and Peace'. It was founded in 1990 by an Arab pastor called George Kazoura and his wife. The majority of the children being cared for in this Christian home are from a Muslim background. Next to the orphanage is a Baptist church where George is the pastor. Since 1998 George has seen over two thousand five hundred people come to the Lord in his church. Many have been healed, some of cancer. But there is also another dimension to George's life . . . he loves the Jewish people. And this is surprising because in 1948 when the State of Israel was declared and there was war in the land, George and his family lost their home in Haifa when they fled to Nazareth and a Jewish family moved in and took their place. This tipped the young George Kazoura into years of anger, bitterness and a desire for revenge.

I was born in the land of Israel and was raised as a child in the city of Haifa in a Catholic Arab family.

In 1948, during the War of Independence, we became refugees. Nobody actually told us to leave, but believing the rumours and out of fear for our lives, we hurriedly fled from our home in Haifa and went north to Nazareth, where there was a large Arab community, and we stayed there for a month until the war was over. Then we packed our few belongings and made our way back to Haifa and to the street where we lived. When we reached our home, much to our surprise and horror we found a Jewish family living there. We explained to them that this was our home. But they did not believe us. They had burnt all our belongings and removed all trace of our ownership of the house. We were left helpless and homeless; on the street, without anything and with nowhere to go. I had five brothers and sisters. In one month, our lives had been turned upside down.

As a child I could not understand how God could love one nation more than another; how he could love one people and throw the others out onto the street. And in no time at all I'd set myself against God and against the Jews. But this was no passive resistance; I became an enemy of God and the Jewish people. I wanted their destruction.

Sad, angry and bewildered, we moved to Nazareth, to be near our relatives, and there we built one room, measuring 25 square metres. This room became our sitting-room, bedroom, dining-room and shower-room – there were eight of us in the family so you can imagine how crowded we were. We were reduced to living in primitive and cramped conditions. As time went on, this situation made me more and more angry towards God and the Jewish people. My character changed from being an easy-going, happy boy to an embittered teenager with only one ambition – to have revenge on the people who had caused me and my family such distress and hardship.

One day I went to visit a friend of mine in Nazareth. When I arrived at his house I was invited in and discovered there were some other people there that I knew, four friends from a Muslim background and three from a Christian background (I must make it clear that in those days, and little has changed, you came from a Muslim or a Christian family background . . . there was and is no middle ground! Rather like today, everybody had a label!). Somebody suggested that we went to a meeting organised by the local communist party. After a brief discussion we all agreed and over the weeks we got quite involved with this group. I learnt about communism and atheism and I liked what I heard because it fuelled my feelings for revenge and desire for justice against those who had destroyed my life. Over the years my heart became even more hard against God and against the Jewish people. Then on 10 October 1961 something happened that was to re-set the course of my life once again.

A week of revival meetings was being held in Nazareth and somebody invited me to go along. I promised to go, but never went. Towards the end of the week, on 10 October, it was a Saturday, my father tried to persuade me to go to the meeting. After a long discussion I told him that I did not want to be an idiot and be like people who believe in a God who loves Jews but hates Arabs. This was the first time I had spoken harshly to my father who, together with my mother, became believers in 1952. We couldn't agree so I left home and went to see my friends.

I discussed the matter with my friends and persuaded them that we should go to the revival meeting and create a disturbance. At first they refused but then we voted and the majority voted to go and disrupt the meeting.

We agreed that we would sit at the front, but when we arrived the church was packed and the only space was on the back row. We found some Bibles on the chairs and started to play with them to make a noise. Somebody asked us to be quiet. This made us angry and we made even more noise! We carried on like this for 90 minutes but nobody told us to be quiet or took any notice of us! This disturbed my heart! Why did nobody take any notice of us?! During the 90 minutes I did not listen to a word the missionary speaker said but in the ninety-first minute the missionary started to ask some questions. 'Do you have peace with God? Do you have peace with your family? Where will you spend eternity?' Then he read a Bible verse. 'What good will it be for a man if he gains the whole world, yet forfeits his soul?' (Matthew 16:26, NIV).

This was the first time I had heard such questions being asked and they went straight into my heart. This caused turmoil in my mind as all the communism and atheism I had believed in rose up to challenge these new ideas. The missionary invited anyone who wanted to begin a new life with Jesus to respond by raising a hand or going to the front.

I felt a great power taking me from my chair and moving me forward, but then I felt somebody catching me from behind and whispering in my ear: 'Don't believe these things. All these things are lies. Did you forget what the Jews have done to you? How can you believe in God, who threw you onto the streets so now you live a miserable life?'

The fight was so fierce in my heart that I could not stay in my place. I left the church with my friends and went home.

When my mother saw me coming home early at about 10 p.m. she asked me what had happened to make me come home so early looking so miserable! She asked me if I'd been in a fight or whether I'd done something wrong! I told her nothing had happened to me and switched on the radio to listen to some loud music. It was unusual for me to turn on the radio and listen to loud music so my mother came to me again and accused me of lying. Without thinking I said, 'I don't know if your Jesus can help me.'

For my mother, to hear me say these words was the high point in her life! She reached for her Bible and sat beside me saying, 'Please read this passage from the Bible; and now this . . . ' When she was young the schools were only for rich people so she didn't learn how to read and write, but she knew many Bible verses by heart. After three hours she brought me to the Old Testament and I read these verses from Isaiah 1:18–20:

'Come now, let us reason together,' says the LORD. 'Though your sins are like scarlet, they shall be as white as snow; though they are red as crimson, they shall be like wool. If you are willing and obedient, you will eat the best from the land; but if you resist and rebel, you will be devoured by the sword.' For the mouth of the LORD has spoken. (NIV)

Then she encouraged me to read from the New Testament, from 1 John 1:9:

If we confess our sins, he is faithful and just and will forgive us our sins and purify us from all unrighteousness.
(NIV)

When I had read these two passages from the Bible, I felt a
great power take me from my bed. I knelt down and started to confess all my sins, one after the other. When eventually I said, 'Amen,' my mother asked me if I really was
George! I told her that the George whom she had known
had died. I was never to be the same again.

In the following ten months I read the Bible from cover
to cover. I worked out that if I read three chapters a day, I
could finish it in ten months. And I did. However, I didn't
find Jesus because, as I now realise, I read it as a secular
history book; my mind had been so full of atheism and
communism. I became disillusioned and decided to rejoin
the communist party. But at the same time I heard another
voice encouraging me to read the Bible again. So I picked
it up and four days later I came to the twelfth chapter of
Genesis where God says to Abraham in verse 3: 'I will
bless those who bless you, and whoever curses you I will
curse; and all peoples on earth will be blessed through
you' (Genesis 12:3, NIV). I started laughing aloud and I
shouted, 'What blessing can come from this man, who
died many thousands of years ago?'

'God,' I shouted, 'if you really are God and these words
are yours, reveal yourself to me and tell me what meaning
it has for me.'

Desiring to be alone, I left the room that we called home. It
was 3 a.m. I was waiting to hear from God. I was very quiet
and sat silently for more than half an hour. Then I felt a hand
on my shoulder. I looked round thinking my mother had

come looking for me. But there was nobody there. Then I heard a voice: 'I am Jesus, who came to earth as a man of flesh, from the seed of Abraham, and I am a Jew, who died for your sins. I forgive you all your sins and I forget them. Now you must forgive your Jewish brothers as I have forgiven you.'

The night came to an end and it was time for me to go to work. The day passed and later that evening I knew what I had to do.

I found my way to our old house and stood outside and forgave the Jews who lived there for what they had done to my family. I extended my hand towards the house and asked God to bless the family who lived there. It was very hard for me to do this, but it was so good for me because immediately I felt a load lift off my back and a joy rising up inside me that I had never experienced before. All the hatred, bitterness and anger that I had felt towards the Jewish people disappeared and from that moment until today, the Jews are no longer my enemies, they are my beloved people. This was a great lesson in my life . . . to forgive, to forget and to be reconciled.

Today a Messianic fellowship meets in that house! Some time later I met an old Jewish man in that congregation. When he heard my story he asked my forgiveness. This simple act touched my heart and immediately I was able to love the Jewish people even more!

And since then, God has blessed me. It's a great honour to be a servant of Christ. And he's given me a precious wife; she understands that my priority is to serve the Lord. And we have four children who all love the Lord.

So much has happened since then . . . and it hasn't always been easy. In 1975, I fell on my back and for three years I couldn't move. I was offered an operation but told that it could be risky and there was a chance I could end up in a wheelchair, unable to walk. So I prayed, and the Lord healed me.

We opened the House of Love and Peace for children from the streets in 1990. It hasn't been easy but we have lived by faith and trusted the Lord for everything. The children we care for are mainly from Muslim families. Many have been taught to kill and throw stones. Here they are taught how to love Israelis. Life seemed to be going well; I can't say it was easy, but we were living by faith and trusting God to help us each day. I thought my attitude was good but in 1998 the pain in my back returned. I visited a chiropractor who told me that it was a serious problem and I needed an operation. But again I was warned that there were risks involved, there was only a 75 per cent chance of success, it would be a ten-hour operation; I would have to spend two months in hospital and it was very expensive. What was I to do?

Again, I prayed. A friend put me in touch with a surgeon in Germany who happened to be an expert in back problems. He looked at my X-rays and agreed that there were great risks involved in the operation, but he offered to do the operation free of charge. The date was set and I travelled to Germany.

The day before the operation, all the tests were re-done and the surgeon was happy. On the morning of the operation I was wheeled down to theatre and given an anaesthetic and the operation started. But after five minutes I died. Whilst the surgeon was giving me electric shock treatment to try and revive me (he later told me!), the Lord took me to heaven. Jesus met me. 'Please, my son, come inside.' Jesus took me to a library and I saw a book. He opened the book to an empty page. 'George, many times you go to serve me but you don't talk about me.'

I was shocked. I begged the Lord to send me back so that I could go and tell the people in my town and country about Jesus.

The surgeon, who was a Muslim, was very relieved when I started to breathe again, but he was very shocked to hear what had happened to me!

That experience radically changed the way I work and speak. Today I have seen over two thousand five hundred people come to the Lord in our church, many from a Muslim background. And I have seen many people healed, including healed from cancer.

I tell them that it all starts with forgiveness and forgetting. We have a verse in this church, '"Not by might nor by power, but by my Spirit," says the LORD Almighty, (Zechariah 4:6, NIV).

In this area (northern Israel) this verse means life to us because Druze and Muslim people have tried to kill Christian Arabs living around here. In some villages, houses and shops owned by Christians have been burnt down.

Today I cannot keep quiet. I teach my Arab congregation about the importance of loving our Jewish neighbours and being a blessing to Israel. I teach the whole Bible. There is no place for a Palestinian Theology, or for Replacement Theology. We have to understand that God loves us all the same, and for his own reasons he has chosen Israel and the Jewish people to reveal himself to the world. We cannot argue with God. He knows what he's doing and we fight him at our peril.

Chapter Four

Labib Madanat

Executive Secretary of the Palestinian Bible Society

Labib's attitude to life in Israel and the Middle East and his role in it is one of the most positive I have heard. He believes that God is at work in the Middle East in general and in Israel in particular, bringing his plan to fulfilment; Labib is working tirelessly, as an Arab Christian, to fulfil his part in that.

He's held his position as Executive Secretary of the Palestinian Bible Society for 12 years so he is well established, knows what he's doing and where he's going. He actually gave up a promising and lucrative career in Jordan to return to the Old City of Jerusalem, where he was born, to work for the Palestinian Bible Society. It was a challenging decision and one he didn't take lightly. But he hasn't looked back and is encouraged at the speed of progress in many areas, as this story will reveal.

The Bible Society has two offices in Jerusalem: an Israeli office and a Palestinian office. I am pleased to be able to report that they work closely together, share the same goals and co-operate on many projects.

What follows is Labib's story . . . it is a personal journey that has profound and far reaching implications for the entire Middle Eastern region. It again proves that God is more interested in

*one man who is obedient to him than an army of people follow-
ing their own agenda. So who is Labib Madanat and where does
he come from?*

   *Labib was born into a Jordanian family. His father was a pas-
tor in Jerusalem so although Labib has lived most of his life
amongst Palestinians he also holds an Israeli ID card! In other
words, he moves freely between Palestinians and Israeli Arabs
and Jews, speaks fluent Arabic, Hebrew and English and has
travelled extensively. Whilst he was brought up in the Old City
of Jerusalem, he eventually went away to study, and this is
where we start his story.*

The streets of the Old City of Jerusalem are a constant
reminder of my childhood when I used to walk with my
dad to the meetings in our church. My father was originally from Jordan, and for a time we lived there too. But in
1981, after finishing my schooling, I went to Iraq, to Mosul
in the north of the country, to study, and stayed there for
four years in Iraq studying agriculture, soils and irrigation.

   At that time I didn't have any ambition to work in a
church and be a pastor like my father. Rather I wanted to
stay in my chosen field of agriculture and irrigation which
I really loved. There was no fellowship where I was studying in Iraq so I had to depend on my own private daily
time of Bible-reading and prayer, and I avidly read
Christian books and witnessed to students around the university. I think those years of isolation as a Christian were
the years of growth in my spiritual life. On leaving Iraq, I
went to university in Jordan where I did a Masters degree
and I was considering doing a doctorate. I thought I had
my career plan neatly worked out, but God had other
plans.

One day I received a request to return to Jerusalem. An elder in the church in Jordan said, 'Labib, our church in Jerusalem needs help. Would you consider going back to serve in the church there?' This request really cut across my plans. So I decided to start praying about it and the more I prayed, the more the desire grew inside me until the time came for me to return to Jerusalem and serve God here.

It sounds quite a radical decision, but at the time it didn't feel that way because I had hopes that maybe I could serve the Lord and still stay in my field. And it felt like the Lord accepted me with that hesitation. However, what actually happened was interesting because when I came here I could not find a job in the area of irrigation or soils. I was busy helping in the church but at the same time I was looking for this other work! I felt certain that the Lord would not expect me to turn my back on all my studies. Then one day I felt the Lord ask me, 'When you dedicated your Master's thesis to me,' as I did literally, 'were you serious or were you joking?' I said, 'Lord, it's all yours.' And then I took the decision that even if I couldn't work in agriculture I was here to stay and serve the Lord and do whatever he asked of me. Shortly after that, the opportunity at the Bible Society opened up for me.

This was a new challenge and quite unexpected. God knew what he had to do within me to prepare my heart and mind for such a job. While I was in Iraq, God baptised my heart with love for the Muslim people. It broke my heart when I saw how the Muslims were killing each other on both sides of the war between Iran and Iraq. Hundreds and hundreds of thousands were brutally murdered on both sides in the name of Islam. And then, when I came to

Jerusalem, during the first few months here, I encountered many Israeli soldiers, and with the little Hebrew that I'd acquired then I told them about Jesus, Yeshua. As they checked my ID I would talk to them and I found that God gave me what I can only describe as a divine love for the Jewish people; love that is not dependent on whether the person in front of you is worthy of this love or not – that was irrelevant. This love was about loving them as people. I just loved them.

Many people might find that hard to understand because they think that for somebody with a Jordanian or Palestinian background, to love Israeli soldiers is quite unusual! But when we Christians mention the word 'love', it's different from how the world understands this word. For us, love equals the cross of Jesus Christ. For the world outside, love has been confused with too many things. So we need to differentiate and talk about the love that we have received from the Father through Jesus Christ. And I believe there are two aspects to this love. Firstly, the Bible teaches us that God's image is in every human being regardless of how evil they might be. This fact alone means that people are able to love and forgive. Hence, even among non-believers you'll see examples of forgiveness, mercy and love wherever there are political or ethnic divides in the world, not only here. That this happens is like a sign of hope from God that he hasn't given up on humanity. But perhaps the second aspect of this love is even more significant; if Christ dwells in my heart then I can love a Jew, a Muslim, a Christian – anybody. This love is unconditional. It means I can love my supposed enemy.

And so my thinking was developing fast. With the changes that were taking place within my heart and mind,

I began to see what God was calling me to do in those early days of my new job; I wanted the Muslims to taste Jesus and the Jews to see him. 'Whatever it takes, Lord,' I prayed, 'whatever it takes to help a Muslim have a taste of how good the Lord is.' And they need to taste; they need to have some sort of an experience which requires them to know us as people, as Christians, not only by our words, but by our lives. For Jewish people, it is easier because when I share my testimony with them and tell them quite simply that I am an Arab whose heart has been changed by the blood of Jesus, they can see that I do not hate them and wonder how this can be.

I had to learn the most effective way of letting Muslims 'taste' Jesus and today I can describe it in these two sentences. 'To live and give. To serve and proclaim the word of God.' You see, you need to come close to people, to live among them. It is not a case of me descending with my religion. It's not a fight between the Bible and the Koran and who will twist the other's arm; that's not the essence of the message of Jesus. The essence of the message of Jesus is that 'God so loved the world'. That is the motivation. The motivation is not anti-Koran, anti-Islam, or anti-Muslim. The motivation is absolute love for a lost human soul, wanting that soul to come back to the Father to meet Jesus and rest in his arms. Nothing less. That is the motivation and it has to be pure, for there is no greater love than this, that somebody should lay down his life for his friends. What can I do to bless the Muslims? How do I live in humility? Do I say 'Forgive me' when I'm wrong? Do I care for their lives as much as I can? Do I live in honesty among them? And how much do I tell them about the love of Jesus? I must not hide it. It is sharing Christ with them in word and deed. I must not live with them for ten years saying nothing about the love of Jesus. No. It all goes together. It's one package. You cannot slice it into pieces and phase it into different stages. Arabs in general are fed up with decades of empty promises from many leaders; they are tired of deferred hopes. So giving them words only is not enough. I do believe in the power of the word of God, but we cannot hide behind it and say the word and the Spirit will do the job. We are responsible to live the word and speak the word and be used by the Holy Spirit so Muslims can taste and see how good the Lord is.

And then, what about the Jewish people? How can I help them to see their Messiah? It is a unique position for an Arab going to a Jew to talk to him about the Jewish Jesus. I assure you we can get their full attention! I remember this story. Once I was invited, as Director of the Palestinian Bible Society, by the Palestinian Ministry of Culture to take part in an international book fair in Tunisia. So I went there on behalf of the Bible Society and we had a display of our Christian books and Bibles and we were the only Christian presence there under the Palestine section. The Saudis were on one side, the Libyans on another side, the Iranians were there . . . and there we were from the Palestinian Bible Society. I was staying at a hotel in Tunis and when I arrived I wanted to get something to eat but they said, 'Sorry, we don't have anything.' I asked, 'Why?' They said, 'The hotel is kosher.' I said, 'I am in Tunis, I am not in Mea Shearim in Jerusalem!' They said, 'No, you don't understand, there's a Jewish group here.' (It was Pesach, Passover). And so I looked and saw a group of Jews, so I started talking to them in Hebrew! They were very surprised that an Arab in Tunis would go and talk to them in Hebrew! And I started telling them about my faith. One of them came to me and said, 'You're almost a Jew!' and we had a beautiful talk together. Consequently, he no longer saw me as an enemy because God's love breaks barriers. So what I am saying is there is extra power and strength when we cross the divide of hostility and animosity, hatred and bitterness, with the message of Jesus. I pray that believers will not miss these opportunities because they are blinded by the political and national problems and challenges, but instead see what God wants us to do in the midst of this horrible situation. God's love transforms us from the position of victims to servants. I've had so many encounters like this! They always end with a sense of blessing and healing.

There is a very real sense that Arab Christians with this perspective really hold a vitally important key in unlocking God's purposes in this part of the world.

To me it is obvious why God allowed both people to be together in the land here. And we need to ask ourselves, what is God's agenda? And even if we differ in our understanding of the biblical prophecies and the end times and all the arguments surrounding the 'theology' of the land I always say, 'Prophecies are God's to fulfil; commandments are mine to obey.' And there are clear commandments for me: love your neighbour like yourself and take the gospel to the whole world, starting from Jerusalem.

God is doing so much amongst the Palestinians these days. I am humbled by the depth and the width of openness within Palestinian society for the true gospel of Jesus Christ. In Gaza the Lord is opening so many opportunities both in the refugee camps and in other very, very difficult areas. He's providing partnership for us to work with many local organisations helping women, children and old people. Similar things are happening in the West Bank. It's good news . . . so many people are receiving Christ. So many Palestinians are dedicating their lives for the love of the Saviour and following him. It is such a huge responsibility. I obviously can't go into too many details. But this is not just wishful thinking. Even now, as we talk, let me give you one example of an opportunity we have. The Palestinian Ministry of Education has granted a local Christian ministry in Bethlehem approval to distribute the Samaritan's Purse shoebox gifts (the Operation Christmas Child) to some maybe eleven to twelve thousand children mostly from Muslim families in south West Bank. No literature is allowed to be distributed, naturally, for children, but they asked us, through our children's ministry programme, Operation Palestinian Child, to perform a programme for those kids. So now we have ahead of us one whole month, as a Christian organisation, of performing a programme for eleven thousand Palestinian children in south West Bank. What a huge responsibility we have – and this is just one opportunity. So the picture is very encouraging, very promising. It is such a thrill and encouragement and uplifting experience to minister, to live and give, to proclaim the word of Christ to the Palestinian people. And the future? I see many more being saved. I see a strong church. I see a shift from a Christian background-based church to a majority Muslim background-based church. This is the picture I see for the Palestinians.

Finally, I would say to the church in the west, be in tune with the heartbeat of the Father. Do not be distracted by politics. You can never change the heart of God from being a Father's heart. He will always love Arabs and Jews the same. His love will always be the same and he wants the church to carry the same heart so his love can flow freely through the church to both peoples.

Chapter Five

Yousef Dakwar

**'Enmity and hostility are living and growing inside you
and you need to do something about it.'**

*When I first met Yousef, I asked him how he liked to be
described and this is what he said: 'Married to a beautiful wife
. . . her name is Christine; she's an Arab from Haifa. We have
three children, a daughter and twins! I too was born in Haifa
although our parents were originally from a village close to the
Lebanese border in Israel, in Galilee. I've been a pastor since
1992. I started a church in the Ramla district of Tel Aviv, and
in the last two years we've started a new church here in Haifa
called the New Covenant Church. We started with six believers – three couples – today we have 70 people! I'm also running
a radio station.'*

*And those few sentences perfectly sum up the man who is
Yousef Dakwar; a self-effacing man who loves his family, lives for
his work; a visionary. I first set eyes on him on a wet day in Haifa
in the middle of winter. We had arranged to meet at the Holiday
Inn Hotel which is set high up overlooking the harbour. If you've
never been to Haifa you have to understand that it's built on the
side of a mountain; the roads leading up from sea-level are very*

steep. On this particular day it was raining so hard, the roads had turned into waterfalls. Indeed, driving had become almost impossible. Stood in the hotel foyer, I saw Yousef arrive in his car. The windows were steamed up and the windscreen wipers were unable to deal with the torrential rainfall. He was peering over his steering wheel as he drove up to the front of the hotel. Beside him was his son and they had come to take my husband and I to see the radio station situated in down town Haifa.

And so we drove off, in the rain, along the flooded roads. Yousef wasn't in the least bit bothered by the inclement weather; he was genuinely delighted to be taking us to see a vision that had become a reality . . . his radio station.

What follows is the story of how this man has overcome hardship, prejudice, persecution and hatred to become an Arab Christian pastor with a heart not only for his own Arab/Palestinian people, but also for Israel and the Jewish people. However, it is a credit to Yousef and others like him that more and more Arab Christians (some are former Muslims) are learning to love the Jews and believe that God's eventual plan for Israel, which when viewed through secular eyes appears unlikely, will happen, to the surprise of the whole world.

Yousef takes up the story . . .

My father originally came from a village near the Lebanese border called Berram, which means 'fruitful', and in those days most of the people living there were farmers. In 1948, the State of Israel was founded and on 13 November of that year, an order came to the people of the village of Berram, via some Israeli soldiers, saying that they should evacuate the village and start walking towards the Lebanese border. The people started to move away, but some were suspicious of this order and were reluctant to go too far. They did not trust the Israeli soldiers as they had heard reports from other Arabic villages in Galilee who had been asked to evacuate their villages only to find they had been destroyed. So these people decided to hide in the woods and in the caves of the surrounding valleys, from where they could watch their village. They had no food or clean water and after a few days seven children died from hunger and thirst; their only consolation was that they died looking at their village in the distance with hope in their hearts that they would soon be able to return. But the weather had turned cold and these children had insufficient shelter. My father witnessed these events. He watched those children die.

After two weeks the Minister for the Minorities (an Israeli government minister responsible for minority groups such as Arabs) came to the village along with the village priest, and they started to call the people together because the minister wanted to speak to them.

This call was like a trumpet call of resurrection! Suddenly all the people started to appear from between the trees. The minister told them that they need not be afraid because they were being asked to evacuate the village for their own protection. And he asked them again to leave, this time for two weeks, and not to take any of their belongings because they would soon be able to return. He explained that this was for their own safety as the war between Israel and Lebanon was putting their lives at risk.

And so on 19 November 1948 the whole village moved away, taking no covers or tents because they trusted this minister and believed they would soon be back.

These simple people took their chickens, cows and sheep and went to another village nearby. And from then, until today, they have never returned to their land. It was really very hard for my father, and grandfather, and for the entire family, to understand why this happened to them. They received promises from the Israeli government that they would be able to return, but these promises were never realised.

I was born in 1969. I remember when I was a child, my father used to take me to his village to sit beside his house which by then lay in ruins; razed to the ground by Israeli aeroplanes which came and destroyed the whole village. Now just broken stones are there. These people didn't put up a fight; they were Israeli citizens with Israeli identity cards; all of them were Christians – but this kind of politics hurt them a lot. They lost their land – thousands of acres, their houses – everything, and they had to start all over again. So for the past fifty or sixty years, these people and their children have been rebuilding their lives.

After these people lost their land, their hearts became full of enmity and hatred towards the Jewish nation and Jewish people. When my father took me to see where his house used to be, he would sit on the stones and cry. They were poor . . . it would have been no more than one room housing eight people with their animals . . . their cows and chickens . . . poor people. But they lost all that they had. So this story lodged in my heart. It made me angry and gradually hatred took root in my heart towards the Jewish people . . . why did they take our land?

My attitudes were also being shaped by my mother. She came from a Catholic background. I used to ask her, 'Who killed Jesus?' 'Who crucified Jesus?' And she would tell me: 'The Jews killed him.' So my understanding of the Jewish people was shaped by these events . . . they took my house, they destroyed my village and they killed my God. My wife came from a similar background, and so together, we felt a lot of bitterness towards the Jewish people.

By the time I was born, my parents had settled in Haifa and I was sent to an Arab Catholic Latin school. I was brought up a Catholic. It's not easy to handle hatred, but when I became a Christian several years later, the Lord revealed to me that there was a really dark side in my heart towards the Jewish people. It was true, they hurt us. It was true they took what little we had and they brought much pain to us and our relatives. But as a Christian I knew I had to deal with this hatred and learn to love.

It happened like this. In 1987 I went to a youth conference with one aim in mind – to find a girlfriend! I went just for fun. However, the Lord touched my heart in one of the meetings and I started weeping and asking the Lord for forgiveness. For three days I wept and wept and wept, pleading with the Lord to forgive me. It was a time of salvation and repentance. I came back to my city a changed man and immediately started searching for the true believers. They were the people I most wanted to be with. As time went on, the Lord showed me that there was something in my heart that I needed to deal with. He showed me that I had a deep hatred towards Israel and the Jewish nation. Gradually, I started to understand a verse from Ephesians chapter 2 where the phrases, 'He put to death their hostility' and 'one new man' spoke to my heart.

As I prayed about this the Lord asked me, 'Do you know why the Bible says "put to death their hostility"?' I prayed and prayed and the Lord said to me, 'Can you put to death a chair?' I said, 'No, there is no life in it.' 'Can you put to death a computer or a table?' I said, 'No.' He said,

'Enmity and hostility are living and growing inside you and you need to do something about it.'

I came to understand that when Jesus put enmity to death, he put to death something that was living. And so, over a period of time I prayed and asked the Lord to put to death the enmity that was living in me. After that, everything changed in my life and I started to pray for the salvation of the Jewish people and I forgave everything they had done to me and, along with my wife, eventually became part of a Messianic Jewish congregation! It was quite a journey!

When I was first saved in 1987 I was eighteen years old. I used to practice Kung Fu and other Eastern fighting techniques. Everybody in my neighbourhood knew me as a tough guy at that time . . . nobody succeeded if they tried to make trouble for me! I was full of anger which energised me and made me want to be strong and violent. After I was saved, I spent a month on my own, reading my Bible and praying and consequently didn't see any of my friends. I only wanted to be with Christians and I went from meeting to meeting to meeting.

When my old friends eventually met me and heard how I had changed, they discussed the matter between them and decided that I, as one of their friends, had lost my way and they should go and get me back! So they caught me in the street and they started rebuking me and cursing me and for the first time in my life I didn't fight back. I just didn't react to what they were saying or what they were doing. After an hour, I asked them if they would like to know what had happened to me. And they said 'Yes, OK, what's happened?' So I started to share with them how I got saved and what the Lord did and how he baptised me in the Holy Spirit and all these kind of things, including the changes he had brought about in my heart and in my life. They were really shocked. They didn't know what to say. Then, they came under conviction and asked me what they should do. And there in the street I told them that they needed to repent. 'How and when?' they asked. 'Here and now,' I replied. And so, that night in the main street in Haifa, five people knelt down and   started to pray for salvation and forgiveness and they were crying. I had only been a believer for one month! I didn't know any verses from the Bible; all I knew was what had happened to me – but the Lord used me to bring them to the faith.

However, my father was not pleased with me when I became a Christian; he really attacked my faith. He threw me out of his house. Many times I slept outside; sometimes I was able to sleep in the homes of other believers, but other times I had to sleep in the street. For him the Catholic Church was the real thing. He accused me of no longer being a Christian. He said my new found faith was demonic. 'We are Catholics, we should keep the faith,' he said. He often threw me out of his house, and there was a lot of trouble.

During that time I was studying at the university to become a radiologist. One day my father said, 'OK, if you leave your faith I will pay your fees for the next four years. If you don't leave, I'm not prepared to pay you one shekel.'

I was a young man, just nineteen years old. I'd already started the course and was keen to qualify as I was thinking of my future and earning a living. But now I had to decide between my faith and my studies. I remember how much I prayed. Then I went to my father and told him how grateful I was that he had taken care of me for nineteen years, but I couldn't leave Jesus because of him; and so I left the university and found a job.

But I didn't feel full of despair because almost immediately I felt drawn to become a worshipper and a pastor. I was already a musician and used to play in a band in the hotels and bars. In fact the friends I've just told you about who were converted one month after me, were my music team. We used to play secular music together but when they got saved we started a new worship band called the Angels. Actually we were called the Angels when we played secular music! So our name didn't change – just the music!

In 1991 the issue of reconciliation really became a central part of my life when I heard that there were Jewish believers who felt the same way and wanted to be reconciled to Arab Christians. I visited several of their congregations, and invited them to our churches. We started to build relationships . . . in the beginning it was very, very hard because it wasn't always easy to understand each other. However, today we celebrate Christmas together and we celebrate Pesach together. I haven't changed . . . I'm still an Arab but we are learning to differentiate between our traditions and our faith. Our faith tells us that we are brothers . . . all sons of Abraham. If you study the Bible it is clear that both Jews and Arabs are sons of Abraham; the Arabs through Ishmael. But the Arabs need to come under the promises of God to Abraham. The Lord says in Isaiah 19, that there will be a highway from Egypt through Israel to Syria and I believe the Arabic world, in the end, will come back to their Messiah and we will start worshipping the same Messiah, Jesus Christ. In the same way, the Jewish nation needs to understand about Jesus. The early church, which was mainly Jewish, was very clear on this . . . they managed to embrace their new faith in Jesus as well as keeping their traditions. I believe all of Israel will be saved eventually.

I realise I am one of a small number of Arab pastors who teach this to their people. What I believe is what the Bible says! We should not negotiate with God's word. It's something we need to accept. We need to make the difference between politics and faith. For example, many believers in the world love Israel and they want to support Israel. So when they see planes or tanks hitting the Palestinians, destroying their homes and villages, they think, well the Jews are God's people, we should be behind that. I don't look at things that way. We should always remember the story in Luke chapter 9:

And he sent messengers on ahead, who went into a Samaritan village to get things ready for him; but the people there did not welcome him, because he was heading for Jerusalem. When the disciples James and John saw this, they asked, 'Lord, do you want us to call fire down from heaven to destroy them, even as Elijah did?' But Jesus turned and rebuked them. And he said, 'You do not know what kind of spirit you are of, for the Son of Man did not come to destroy men's lives, but to save them.' And they went to another village.

(Luke 9:52–55, NIV)

How can we as believers pray for the destruction or fall of a nation; how can we support killing and war? We should always know what manner of spirit is influencing us: 'for the Son of Man did not come to destroy men's lives, but to save them.'

I believe in the salvation of the Jewish nation. I believe the promises of God do not change and we need to believe them, but I do not agree with what the Israeli politicians are doing to my people. But that does not mean I should be their enemy. And let's remember that on the other hand, we are hurting the Jews. As an Arab I do not agree with what the Palestinian leaders are doing towards the Jewish people. The Bible has much to say about the life and faith of Abraham. He was the first man to receive the promise from God that he and his seed would inherit the land. In Hebrews the Bible says about Abraham:

> By faith he made his home in the promised land like a stranger in a foreign country; he lived in tents, as did Isaac and Jacob, who were heirs with him of the same promise. For he was looking forward to the city with foundations, whose architect and builder is God. . . . All these people were still living by faith when they died. They did not receive the things promised; they only saw them and welcomed them from a distance. And they admitted that they were aliens and strangers on earth. People who say such things show that they are looking for a country of their own. If they had been thinking of the country they had left, they would have had opportunity to return. Instead, they were longing for a better country – a heavenly one. Therefore God is not ashamed to be called their God, for he has prepared a city for them.
>
> (Hebrews 11:9,10,13–16, NIV)

What do these verses mean? Abraham was promised the earthly, material things in the land . . . which he got. But his heart was not on earth, it was in heaven – he looked forward to the heavenly city and this attitude should be ours also. We fight for land... but we cannot take it with us when we die. So all the enmity comes from fighting over land. I still believe that the land belonged to Abraham's seed. Does that mean the Arabs are outside of this covenant? I don't think so. I believe the Arabs are under God's promises, and the salvation of Israel will not be fulfilled without the Arabs. It's not by mistake that we are here in this land. It's God's plan. God wants to reach those Arabs who have turned away from the real faith to Islam. Six hundred and twenty years after Christ, Muhammad started his religious activity and he has now taken almost one billion people into this religion. Do you know why? Because the church at that time was very weak. It was involved with politics, land and money. And it lost the hearts and minds of the people. And then Muhammad came and started to take an interest in the people and teach them his ideas.

And so the Arabs that we read about in Acts 2, who were in Jerusalem on the day of Pentecost when the Holy Spirit came and the apostles spoke in tongues, gradually slipped away from the faith and 620 years later embraced Islam. I believe this happened because the church did not embrace them; and today, if the church will not love the Arab nations, the Lord will hold us responsible. I believe we will start to see the salvation of Israel when we see Jews and Arabs coming back in their millions to the Lord.

The Lord has shaped my life so much over the years. And also my wife. We knew each other when I was twelve years old . . . she was my neighbour! I shared my faith with her when I was eighteen years old; she was saved, along

with all her family at that time! When I was twenty-three
years old we married.

As I've already mentioned, before I was saved I was
involved in a music band, and over the years, I remained
involved in the music world, in Christian music. One day
I met a man who was involved in an Arabic Christian
television programme. We worked together on a few programmes; he noticed that I was very interested in the
media and, sensing my enthusiasm, offered to pay for me
to go to Canada to get some training in TV and radio pro-
duction.

So I went to Canada in 1997 for a four-month course and
during that time I had a vision of how the media could be
used in the Middle East to spread the gospel. I came back
to Israel and soon after the Lord called me to move from
the Tel Aviv area to Haifa – back to our family home town.
We started to pray asking God to show us why he had
taken me to Canada for four months . . . what should I do
with that training? Five years later, the Lord spoke to my
heart and showed me how the Internet could be used to
reach people in their homes and offices. Many Arabs are
afraid to talk openly about what they believe about God.
But I realised that radio via the Internet could reach deep
into Arab areas, right into their homes and I could tell
them about God. I came back from Canada with so much
energy and excitement. At first I couldn't understand why
the Lord didn't open up an opportunity for me in the
media immediately! Now I understand why! And so now
we have started an Internet radio station called Radio
Altareeq (meaning 'The Way' radio in Arabic), and we
believe we will move into television programmes via the
Internet and satellite too.

When the Lord gave me the name for this radio station, he said, 'I am the way and the truth and the life.' So we knew we had to share this message with the people; that there is a way that is so different from the other ways because it is truth and life. We tell them about Jesus Christ . . . that he is there to meet their needs, to be close to them.

We started this radio station in October 2003. The first month we got 38 hits on our website. By the end of 2004 we got 78,000 hits; since the beginning of 2005 we have been getting between 220,000 and 250,000 hits per month, 98 per cent from Arab countries. I don't understand how the Lord brings all these people to our website, listening to the radio and reading the articles we put there. We get a huge response. A man from Morocco recently emailed to say he wanted to know more about Christianity and Jesus Christ.

So has God finished with Israel? If he has finished with Israel, has he finished with us also? Why should he finish with Israel? They are human beings, they are his people, they need salvation. I believe God gave many promises to his people and I believe the church can share this inheritance. There is no place for Replacement Theology, or Palestinian Theology or any other politically motivated theology. It's quite simple; the Bible makes it clear – every Jew who believes in Christ can be saved and every Arab or Gentile who believes in Christ can be saved. There is also some bad teaching being spoken that it is enough to be a Jew . . . no. If it is enough to be a Jew, why do we need Christ?

> No-one who denies the Son has the Father; whoever acknowledges the Son has the Father also.
>
> (1 John 2:23, NIV)

God's promises will never be changed. He never changes his mind. I pray for my Arab people to be saved and I pray for the Jewish nation to be saved.

I want to see Arabs and Jews and Christians here in Israel meeting in one place worshipping the same God – I dream of big numbers. Why? Because we have the same Father and the same Spirit. We can be 'one new man'.

Chapter Six

Emil Boutros Boktor

'How can you preach about love and yet have great hatred?'

Today Emil is leading a church in Egypt. A former officer in the Egyptian army, the direction of his life changed unexpectedly during the Six Day War of 1967 in the Sinai desert, in what must have looked an apocalyptic scene with thousands of fellow Egyptians lying dead around him. This is the story of a man who quite literally met God and was never to be the same again. His theology changed, his attitudes changed and his work changed from that moment on.

I was raised in a Christian home and my father was a Pentecostal pastor. Although in school we were taught to hate the Jews, in Sunday school and through my dad's preaching in church I learnt that the Jews were the chosen children of God. My father was aware of what I was being taught at school, and so he tried to correct this wrong teaching and redress the balance. My dad preached a lot about the second coming of Jesus Christ. As a curious child, I once asked him if it would ever be

possible for me to visit Jerusalem, the city Jesus is returning to. His response was a resounding 'Yes!' So a visit to
Jerusalem became a childhood dream for me; I longed to
go there.

After my years in school, I started my further education
in Egypt before going on to a Bible school in Belgium
where I took my Masters degree in Theology; then I went
to the US, to the University of Minnesota where I did my
PhD. While I was in Belgium, one of my professors was an
American Jew (from a German background) who, after
discovering that I was an Egyptian, hated and despised
me. He often humiliated me in front of others. This was a
painful experience. He would quote verses from the Old
Testament at me referring to the way the Egyptians
humiliated the Jewish people all those years ago, and in
that way directed his hatred of the Egyptian people
towards me.

After finishing my theological studies, I returned to
Egypt where I planned to work full-time in the ministry,
possibly as a pastor.

In Egypt, military service is compulsory, so . . . I joined
the Egyptian army in 1966. I was due to be released from
my service in July 1967. However, just before I was about
to be released, the Six Day War started, on 5 June 1967 – a
war between Israel and the Arab countries.

The night before that war I was on duty in the Sinai
desert. I was an army officer. I was just nine kilometres
away from Egypt's border with Israel. At 6 a.m., after finishing my duty, I went down to my bunker to rest. In the
midst of all the tension, and as a born-again Christian pastor, I felt a great desire in my heart to pray to the Lord for
peace. I was praying and speaking in tongues, when

suddenly, the Holy Spirit spoke to me: 'The war will come, but I will keep you safe.'

I fell asleep, but two hours later I was suddenly woken by the sound of great explosions close by! I ran outside to discover that Israel had attacked our Egyptian air force base, bombed all our planes and set them all on fire. In what seemed like no time at all, everything had been destroyed. As I watched our planes burning, the entire area resembled a giant furnace; everywhere I looked I saw fire, death and destruction.

Immediately our troops wanted to retreat back towards our own borders. At first I stayed in my place. The men tried to persuade me to return with them. But I said, 'No, I can't do that. I'm an officer, I have to obey orders.' So I stayed in that place for three days along with over five hundred of my men. On the third day I was sleeping in one of the bunkers, hidden from the shooting and the rockets, and I slept for maybe four hours. When I woke up I discovered that all the troops had disappeared. I didn't know what had happened to them or where they had gone. Only seven people remained – sheltering in two bunkers. And so we began to plan how to go back to our country, and left.

Two days later, I heard that the Israeli troops had occupied our land in the Sinai and had surrounded the Egyptian troops and captured many men. To evade capture ourselves, we used to walk during the night and shelter in the bunkers during the day because as well as having troops and tanks on the ground, the Israeli jets used to come and shoot our soldiers as they walked in the desert. I ended up being in the desert for six days.

I'm not sure how it happened but during the third night, as I walked, I felt I'd become separated from the rest

of my group and lost my way. It was 2 a.m. and very dark.
For the first time in my military service I felt fear sweeping over me. To encourage myself I began to sing a song my mother had taught me as a child; a song that tells how lonely days and lonely nights filled with despair makes you long for someone to care for you. Then I heard Jesus speaking to me, giving me a promise: 'Don't be afraid. You will never be lonely again as you have opened the doors of your heart to me.'

Suddenly, as I sang, I saw a tiny light far away in the distance. I hoped it was one of our Egyptian bunkers and walked towards it. The light came closer and closer and got bigger and bigger, until finally it hit my face. I was blinking in the brightness but in the midst of the light I saw Jesus – I knew it was him. He said: 'I will send you back to your country safely. Tell my people in Egypt, and in the whole world, that I love them.' I spent about four hours in the presence of Jesus, the Great God, as if I was in a trance – until the sun rose and its light hit my face.

As Jesus promised, eventually I returned safely to my country – I walked all the way. After Jesus had appeared to me and told me that I would reach my country, I was encouraged and began to walk with a new confidence. But it was a hard experience. My feet were swollen. I was suffering. I took off my shoes and wrapped my feet in clothes and began to walk. It took me another three days. Many of my colleagues had been killed. I saw them lying where they had died there in the desert. I was crawling over their dead bodies to flee the Israeli jets and tanks as they attacked Egyptian troops. I saw many soldiers bleeding, dying, thirsty and hungry on the hot sand of the Sinai desert. And hatred began to grow in my heart. As I was crawling on the ground I saw hundreds of men, many of them were of a high rank; most of them were young men – married or engaged. I saw the wedding rings on their hands. And it touched my heart and I began to think about the situation – why did we have to fight against Israel . . . why did they fight against us . . . why did they shoot at us and kill us . . . and treat us as less than animals? We were so helpless, scattered on the face of the Sinai desert. I could feel hatred rising in my heart towards the Israeli people – why were they doing this?

A few years later, I was at war again – the October 6th War of 1973 (known in Israel as the Yom Kippur War; this war started on 6 October and lasted until 24 October 1973). We crossed the Sinai desert and took the Bar-Lev forts – a strategic Israeli stronghold in the Sinai which they had captured from us during the Six Day War. Again, my heart was scarred with anger and I felt great hatred towards Israel grow within me.

This hatred really took hold of my heart. For many years I decided not to read the Old Testament in my Bible and not to preach or quote verses from the Old Testament in my work as a Christian pastor. So for nine years I only preached from the New Testament – until 1982. Then one Saturday night I was preparing my sermon notes for the following Sunday morning. I was planning to talk about love as it is described 1 Corinthians 13. Suddenly, I felt the Holy Spirit whispering in my ear: 'Are you going to preach about love?' I said, 'Yes, Lord' and he answered me, 'How can you preach about love and yet have great hatred in your heart for Israel?'

I immediately came under conviction and there and then confessed to the Lord about the hatred in my life and how it had consumed my heart and become such a terrible battle within me. I knew I couldn't overcome this hatred in my own strength. I cried out to the Lord, 'Lord if you can heal me – I am here.' I knelt down and began to pray, asking the Lord to heal me. Suddenly, a wave like cold water swept from the top of my head and washed down into the centre of my being. It flowed into my heart and took away my hatred. I felt such a great joy! I was healed!

A few months later, I received an invitation from an Arab pastor in Israel to preach at a convocation, an annual event, organised by the Arabic-speaking churches there. As I landed at Tel Aviv airport I began to cry. I was not only stepping into the land I had always wanted to tread but I was also coming face to face with the fears and ill feelings I had carried in my heart about Israel. I was met at the airport by an Israeli Messianic pastor! He came towards me and we introduced ourselves and then he hugged me and I hugged him. Words were not needed. I cried uncontrollably because now I knew that finally, all trace of hatred was gone from my heart. I knew Jesus had reconciled me to the Jewish people. I was full of praise to the Lord who, when he died on the cross, made it possible for the wall of hostility between the Jews and the Gentiles to be broken down and replaced by forgiveness, reconciliation and peace just as Paul explained to the Ephesians when he wrote to them all those years ago.

When I think back to that convocation in 1982 I can clearly remember seeing and experiencing the breaking down of the walls and the removal of the partition between us when a fellow Egyptian Arab, a Jewish believer and I chose to embrace each other with the love of Christ. It was such a great joy, I could not get over it for days and I cried so hard because I could not believe that such a thing could ever happen to me. I was not only free in my heart and in my spirit but I was also filled with indescribable joy.

I love Jerusalem. I don't know what attracts me to it so much but I especially love the walls of Jerusalem. I love walking around the walls and through the gates of Jerusalem. I love to just spend time talking with the people there inside the gates. Whenever I go to Jerusalem, I go to the Dome of the Rock, kneel with my Arab brothers and rebuke the spirit of Islam. Then I go to the Holy Sepulcher and rebuke the spirit of tradition and religiosity amongst Christians, and I also go to David's Sepulcher and rebuke the religious spirits amongst the Jews. I always go to these three places and pray to God for deliverance. I believe in the Holy Spirit and I believe in the freedom that comes only through the Holy Spirit.

And so today, the Lord has put in my heart a great love for the Jewish people, for Muslims and for Egyptians. Every Sunday, after our morning worship service, we receive at least five hundred Muslims who come to the church for deliverance from sickness and from demon possession. We pray for them and God heals them in the name of Jesus. We give them New Testaments and Christian tapes free of charge. They are eager to find out. They are hungry for God. Many people within our congregation often question me: 'Why do we do this? They are fanatics, they want to kill us, destroy us, and make trouble for us; why do we allow them to come to our church?'

I say: 'We love them. We will pray for them. We will keep praying not just for their healing but also for their salvation. We will do this until Arabs, Jews and the nations of the world come together to worship Jesus as their Saviour and King.'

Since my first visit in 1982, I have returned to Israel many times to preach the word of God from the whole Bible – the New and Old Testaments. And I pray for peace in Jerusalem. I pray for peace in the Arab nations. I pray for peace in my homeland Egypt.

I believe in Isaiah 19:23–25 – that God is going to combine together the three ancient nations of Israel, Egypt and the Assyrians. Today I understand the Assyrian people to be the four nations of Turkey, Syria, Iran and Iraq. So God is going to combine them together with Israel and there will be a highway to Egypt through Israel, and from Israel to Iraq and Iran through the other Arab nations, and he will gather together his people – all those Jews and Arabs who believe that Jesus is going to return to Jerusalem to establish his kingdom. We have so many churches in Egypt against this. But this is what I preach. I have my own live television programme four times every week on a satellite television station that covers 77 nations reaching 250 million Arabic speaking people. We receive a large number of emails and letters from all over the Arabic-speaking world, even from Saudi Arabia – the Lord is touching their hearts. It's started – we have a highway now – God is gathering his people and he's going to establish his kingdom in Jerusalem. And one day, the Lord will reveal himself there as the King of kings and the Lord of lords. That's what I believe; that's what I am teaching.

Chapter Seven

Naim Khoury

'I think we are in the beginning of a revival in this land.'

Naim Khoury is an Arab Christian. Born in the Old City of Jerusalem in 1951, for the past 25 years he's ministered in the West Bank and is the pastor of the First Baptist Church in Bethlehem. More recently he's started a second church, this time in the heart of the Old City of Jerusalem; it's called, quite simply, the Jerusalem Church.

I first met Naim in Jerusalem in April 1999. Since then, he has lived through one of the bloodiest intifadas in Israel's recent history and survived an assassination attempt on his life; fortunately the bullet grazed his upper arm, just missing his heart. And yet, as I listened to the interview recorded a few days after that attack with subsequent, more recent recordings, what strikes me is that his message hasn't changed; neither has his attitude. Listening closely to what he was saying in April 1999, it's obvious he was anticipating trouble between Jews and Palestinians; he was ready for it. He knew, because he's a Bible scholar, that if the Bible is to be believed, that great trouble would come to Israel before the second coming of Jesus (an event which he believes is very close). If there is any discernable difference in the interviews, it is that he is anticipating the second coming of the Messiah even sooner now.

So who and what have shaped the life of this man? He is quietly spoken. He has an engaging smile. His brown eyes are kind. He chooses his words carefully. He is very keen to talk about Jesus – less enthusiastic about describing his own story. And I think the reason for that is, his faith is so real; his belief that Jesus is the Son of God who died on the cross and who three days later rose again and is alive today and who is soon to return is not just an intellectual exercise for Naim; it's his reason for living. It's what motivates his every word and action.

He told me how, since 1999, the past few years of conflict have been 'a difficult time' with 'much opposition' and 'much persecution'. 'Yet,' he told me, 'we have seen God's hand on the ministry. We have never experienced the Lord's blessing so much as in the past three to four years. The church in Bethlehem has doubled in size and the reason why? People are seeking for a better direction, a better life; they have been looking everywhere to find a solution to their personal and spiritual needs and I believe that the only one who can supply that is the Lord Jesus Christ. And that's what I tell them! We've seen the Lord work in a very beautiful way. Many people have come to know the Lord. We've been baptising people almost every month and God has been pouring the power of the Holy Spirit upon us. I think we are in the beginning of a revival in this land.'

I put it to him that many people in the west would be surprised to hear that there is a spiritual revival going on in Israel and the Palestinian areas because we have been hearing on our news reports that economically things are very hard for the Palestinians and many are leaving places like Bethlehem in search of a better life elsewhere.

'Yes, that's true,' Naim agreed. 'Many families have left for Canada and the United States and Australia because the economy is so bad in Bethlehem and they are looking for a better life for themselves and their children. Hundreds of Christians have left Bethlehem in the past few years. Every month I hear of more families who have taken the decision to move away. And I don't blame them. It's very hard here. The impact of the suicide bombers and the bloodshed has been devastating. People have become nervous. The majority have lost their jobs. The tourism industry has collapsed. Shops and businesses have been forced to close. People are hungry. In my church in Bethlehem, 90 per cent of my church members are without work. But I want to add that there is a strong body of Christians amongst the Palestinian people and these Arab people love Jesus in just the same way as you do in the west. They love Jesus with all their hearts and these are the ones we need to look after because they are having a very hard time. I pastor a church of over two hundred people – 90 per cent of them have no job. Some weeks they cannot feed their children. My message to believers in the rest of the world is to understand that not all Palestinians are terrorists; there are many precious Palestinians and Arabs who love Jesus like you do.'

Naim and his wife have four grown-up children, one girl and three boys. Two are studying in the United States. Their eldest son is the pastor of a church in a town five miles north of Jerusalem. Their daughter is a journalist and film producer.

Naim grew up in the Old City of Jerusalem during the days when East Jerusalem was controlled by the

Jordanians. Then in 1967, during the Six Day War, everything changed and Jerusalem was recaptured by the Israelis and came under Israeli government. It is easy to see the aftermath of this war even today, nearly forty years later. Many buildings in East Jerusalem still bear the scars of bullet holes as Jordanian and Israeli soldiers battled, each side determined to hold onto this small yet significant area of land.

Naim's parents belonged to the Greek Orthodox Church. But it clearly hadn't attracted the young Naim. He describes how he 'found the Lord' in his twenties, in the early 1970s just a few years after the Six Day War.

'I am so thankful that I found the Lord in the City of Jerusalem.'

I was intrigued to know how this had happened.

'I'd never read the Bible because I'd never had a Bible. So I was ignorant until one night, at a meeting in the YMCA in West Jerusalem, I listened to a preacher from America describing how Jesus Christ died on a cross for me. That night the Holy Spirit grabbed my heart and I could not leave that meeting without making a decision. And I'm glad I did. I am so thankful to God for what he has done for me.

'However, it was not easy for me to share what I'd done with my friends and family and I kept it secret for a week. Then the Holy Spirit told me I could not keep what had happened to me a secret, I had to share the news with my own people. I thought about this before deciding what to do because I knew it could mean trouble. Then I made up my mind and told the Lord I was willing to do whatever he asked of me. I went home and immediately started to talk to my family about my experience with the Lord, but they did not like what they heard. My parents thought it was awful of me to leave the Orthodox Church and I had a hard time. From being happy at home, I started to experience a lot of difficulties and a lot of persecution. However, because we had always enjoyed a close relationship, I thought that after a month or two they would get over it. But they didn't and the hard times and the persecution lasted for over seven years.

'They treated me badly. They said bad things to me. They prevented me from going out with my friends. It was very hard – as a young man it was very, very hard for me. But thank God, after seven years things started to change. I had been praying for my family, for their salvation, and after seven years my mother came to know the Lord and we started to pray together for the rest of the family. Then over the years, one by one, all my brothers and sisters came to know the Lord as their personal Saviour. Finally after almost twenty-seven years of daily prayer for my last brother, my oldest brother, the Lord touched him too – and that tells us Jesus is in control! It tells us he is the same yesterday, today and for ever, and we are so thankful for that.

'During my younger years I was educated in Jerusalem and then I went to America to study Theology. After graduating I had to decide what to do next. Life in America had its attractions. But the Lord put it on my heart to return home and go to Bethlehem because I had heard there was no real witness in the city. The Lord touched my life which enabled me to go and start a work there and with the Lord's help, we did. We started the church in a two-bedroom apartment where we met for a year. As the numbers grew we realised we needed a larger building so we started to build a church. They were exciting days and when we moved in, the church grew even larger and today we have over two hundred members. As well as the church in Bethlehem, I'm now also pastoring a church in the Old City of Jerusalem called the Jerusalem Church.

'The church in Bethlehem started in 1980 when the city was under Israeli rule. In those days the Christian population in Bethlehem was large. But today, things are quite different. Now Bethlehem is governed by the Palestinian Authority and the conflict of the past five years has affected the economy so severely that every year more and more people are leaving so that today the percentage of the population in Bethlehem who are Christian is very small. Bethlehem depends on tourism, and with no tourists the shops have not been selling any goods, the hotels have been empty and the taxi drivers have had little demand. Consequently the people have become really disappointed. Everybody expected the year 2000 to be flourishing with plenty of work and business. But it wasn't so. Things got worse and worse; nobody could have guessed how bad things would become – that's why people decided to leave and look for better opportunities abroad.'

So why did Naim decide to stay and how come the church has grown if so many Christians have left Bethlehem?

'Yes, we stayed and we thank God that in the midst of all the problems and difficulties the church has almost doubled so that we now have over two hundred people. However, because of the economic situation, along with the growth of the church has come a problem – a huge burden of responsibility on us to help the people and encourage brothers and sisters from all over the world to help. I have been under enormous pressure to care for the people in the church because they have been desperate for food for their children and money to pay their electricity bills. We always hope that some day things will change, and the economy, and both Arabs and Jews can live in peace and harmony together. But it's a challenge. It's hard to watch families you have come to know and love move away from Bethlehem. The place is no longer full of life. People have lost their joy. Many people living in Bethlehem have no hope. That's why I know God wants me to stay here. But I have to be honest: there are a lot of aggravations. It's a military zone; weapons are involved. I understand that the Israelis need to protect themselves to be able to move in and out and that's why we Christians are treated in just the same way as all the other Palestinians – with suspicion. We are not treated as Christians. It doesn't make any difference whether you're a Christian Palestinian or a Muslim Palestinian. If you are a Palestinian you have to go through the same Israeli security procedures . . . we are all treated in the same way. The Israeli soldiers are scared of us Palestinian Christians in the same way as they are scared of the Palestinian Muslims and the Palestinian suicide bombers; to them we are all Palestinians and not to be trusted. It's been and continues to be a very tough time.'

'So, what about the treatment of Palestinian Christians at the hands of militant Palestinian Muslims in Bethlehem?' I asked Naim. He answered me thoughtfully and carefully.

'There are some problems – we expect to have some conflict, some confusion, some disagreement between Christians and Muslims. But, taking an overview of the situation, let's remember that both Christians and Muslims have been living under pressure, and sometimes it's very, very difficult to determine exactly what's going on.'

I put it to Naim that one of the most interesting and probably challenging aspects of his work is the way he has deliberately sought involvement and developed friendly relationships with Jewish believers. I wondered why he had been prepared to do this, especially as he was so challenged, being a Christian and in the minority amongst his own Palestinian people. Do many of his fellow Arab pastors share his enthusiasm for fostering strong links with Israeli believers, and what happened to encourage him down that route in the first place?

'I really discovered that it all depends on the word of God. It's all in the word of God. The position I have come to over the last fifteen years or so is found in the Bible in both the Old and the New Testaments. The more I studied the Bible, the more I discovered that the covenant promises God made with Abraham and his people, are for ever and ever and ever. In the early days of my ministry I did not fully understand these things and so I did not pay them any attention. But more recently I have come to realise that these ancient promises are just as relevant today as they were then. And that discovery really stirred and blessed my heart. These were not my ideas! I read them in God's word. I do not believe that anybody has the authority to change God's word and his promises! No one can switch or twist it – it's God's word and we have to believe it just as it is written. My faith in God's word is my priority. It's the most important thing in my life. If we don't want to put Jesus first above all things, I do not think we can call ourselves believers in God's word or in the Lord Jesus Christ. He said, "I came not to destroy the Law, but to fulfil it." And we have to accept that. Consequently I believe in the biblical promises for God's chosen people, the Jews, and for Israel, the Promised Land, regardless of whether people like it or not; regardless of the political situation – I don't have anything to do with politics. My position is completely based on God's word.'

'But,' I said, 'there are many Palestinian Christians who do not love Israel like you do . . . what do you say to your people about the situation?'

'It breaks my heart to see born again evangelical leaders taking the position of Replacement Theology and being anti-Israel in so many ways; I am talking here of Palestinian Christians living in the West Bank and in East Jerusalem. It breaks my heart because it causes me to break my fellowship with them because I stand on the promises of God to his people and the land of Israel because the covenant was made with his chosen people and it is an everlasting covenant, regardless of the wrong things they are doing now. I believe we should not mix politics with spiritual matters – we cannot see clearly if we do that. Rather I believe we need to keep standing on the promises of God towards his Jewish people until the day when we see these things fulfilled. Because of the present situation and tensions and troubles it's hard for many to believe that these things can ever change. But I believe in the word of God. That's the position I am taking.'

'That may be the position you are taking, but presumably that puts you in the minority within the Palestinian Christian community?'

'Yes, I realise that I am a minority amongst a minority! And because of my position I have been harassed a lot by both Muslims and Christians. Our church has been bombed 14 times over the past ten years. In September 2003 I was shot whilst getting out of my car in our driveway; one bullet went into my left arm and the other two missed me. I have been threatened many times. That means the enemy is working to try and silence me. But there is good news – we have victory in Jesus. It is not yet time for me to die! There are many things that need to be accomplished before Jesus comes back again. So I am not going to give up. I am not going to stop preaching the truth, the whole truth from the word of God, both the Old Testament and the New Testament.

'We are very busy working on a major project to make sure our community has enough food to eat. We have been appealing and requesting a lot of aid for our people – fellow members of the body of Christ who are suffering and who are not able to provide enough food for themselves. We've been trying to buy some food and distribute it to the families who need it most. And there are an increasing number of issues regarding people who need specific medicines and others who require medical attention, but there is not the money available to pay for this. We are asking God's people to open their hearts towards the Palestinians and the Arabs. The wonderful thing is that Jewish believers are trying to help us! They send us what they can, but the needs are so great within Israel too. Not many people in the west realise that the economic situation has thrust so many Jewish people down below the poverty line as thousands of people have lost their jobs and the State cannot afford to pay the necessary welfare.

'I would urge the church in the west to return to the values of the early church; they really had concern for each other, they had compassion, they had love; they did their best to make collections and send it to the church in Jerusalem to help the brothers and sisters who were suffering for their faith in the Lord Jesus Christ in crucial times in a land of conflict, a land of problems and difficulties.

'I never ever felt that we are so close to the coming of the Lord Jesus Christ than in the last three to four years. The Spirit of the Lord is melting the ice as we've seen people coming to know the Lord, even Jews and Muslims. We've seen God move so powerfully in this land that we know we're looking for the coming of the Lord Jesus soon. There has been a change in the spiritual climate in this land recently. Regardless of the opposition, we've seen the change. We've seen the response of the people towards the gospel. Praise God!'

With the heat of the spiritual climate increasing, I asked Naim if he had noticed any increased signs of reconciliation between Jews and Arabs.

'I am so proud to say I am a part of that reconciliation! I enjoy regular fellowship with many Messianic leaders. I've spoken at their conferences and in their congregations. Some people might find it unusual for an Arab pastor to preach to a Jewish congregation! But the Lord is bringing us together. I believe that every single person, whether Jew or Gentile, has to come to the saving knowledge of the Lord Jesus Christ to be able to go to heaven because Jesus said, "I am the way the truth and the life."

'But reconciliation is challenging and can be very difficult unless we, both Jews and Gentiles, grab the Lord Jesus Christ and hold on to the promises of God in his book. That's the only way it can happen. Jesus is the only one

who can bring us and keep us together. This is a movement that transcends politics. I'm not involved in politics
at all. Politics to me are secondary. My main concern, my
vision, my heart, my love is to see people, both Jews,
Arabs and Palestinians, come to know the Lord Jesus
Christ – that's the sweetest thing. I think politics is a very
dirty game because 99 per cent of it is opposed to the word
of God; that's why I don't like mixing politics with God's
word.'

'So what do you say to your own people who have a
problem accepting God's word in the way that you do?' I
asked Naim.

'You see, it takes time. You cannot overcome this problem immediately. You cannot convince them all at once;
rather slowly, slowly. The more people love Jesus and
his word, the more they'll understand and accept his
promises in his word.'

'And are you finding that people are embracing your
teaching?' I asked.

'Oh yes, they love it. And not because I say so. I have
God's word to prove it! We don't pay attention to politics;
those who believe in Replacement Theology base their
beliefs on what politicians say rather than the word of
God. And you cannot do that. You cannot ignore God's
promises in God's word and agree with politicians just
because they are politicians!'

Naim seemed so sure of his position even though it put
him in such a lonely and often dangerous situation. Then
without a moment's hesitation he opened his Bible to
Isaiah 6:8: 'Then I heard the voice of the Lord saying,
"Whom shall I send? And who will go for us?" And I said,
"Here am I. Send me!"' (NIV)

'Isaiah replied, "Here am I. Send me." People need to focus on the word of God. If believers do not know the word of God, it's easy for them to be persuaded by the argument for Replacement Theology, or to be agnostic. And I believe that so much of what politicians say today is rubbish and has nothing to do with God's word. Consequently, the weaknesses found in the thinking of believers today come because they are listening to the politicians and not studying the word of God. They are not spending enough time reading the word of God. They go to church and go home feeling happy; and that's it! I say, unless you fall in love with God's word on a daily basis, you're not going to discover God's plan.

'I believe we are so close to the end of time. In one sense, the trouble all around us really encourages me to keep going because what is happening is really a sign of the end – the Jews returning to the land and the deserts blooming – that should tell us believers something. But if you don't know the word of God, you see all these things and don't understand what's really happening! But the people who know the word of God understand that what is happening is not by chance or accident; God is gradually preparing for the second coming of Jesus Christ, the King of kings and Lord of lords.

'Many of us are reading Isaiah 19:23–25 with excitement. Here is a prophecy that is yet to be fulfilled.

In that day there will be a highway from Egypt to Assyria. The Assyrians will go to Egypt and the Egyptians to Assyria. The Egyptians and Assyrians will worship together. In that day Israel will be the third, along with Egypt and Assyria, a blessing on the earth. The LORD

Almighty will bless them, saying, "Blessed be Egypt my people, Assyria my handiwork, and Israel my inheritance." (NIV)

'Yes, the highway . . . I believe that's what's going to happen – Egypt, Syria and Israel – in God's time we'll see the fulfilment of that prophecy. It will be a blessing to many believers. I am teaching my church members all about God's promises and what is really happening at the moment. Recently I've been teaching them about Revelation and the end times. I want to encourage them to be involved and play their part and role in the end times – that means being brave and broadening their vision, and encouraging them to spread the gospel. It's hard for Arab Christians living in the West Bank to believe these things . . . but more and more are realising that God's word is true and the church is growing despite the hardships and persecution.'

I wondered how much Naim could say about his work with other Jewish pastors? He didn't hesitate.

'Most of my fellowship is with Messianic Jewish pastors because I cannot find many Palestinian pastors who share my understanding of God's word. Most of them hold to the Replacement Theology viewpoint because they are involved in politics; that's why they take that position. They've had meetings and organised more meetings to talk about writing a "Palestinian Theology" and always base this philosophy on the current political scenario rather than on the biblical scenario. It makes me very sad because they are picking and choosing the parts of the Bible they want to believe in and leaving out the rest.

'I think they are spiritually blind. They don't see what God has to say in his word. I've been blessed to be around Messianic Jews and I don't have any problem with that at all. I refute Replacement Theology. I don't teach it. I preach against it and let people know that no one can change God's word.'

'But what about the cost? Aren't you afraid that one day somebody will shoot you and this time not miss?' I asked Naim.

'I believe every time a person decides to take a stand, they should first count the cost. God promises in his word that he will never leave or forsake me and elsewhere it says, his angel "encamps around those who fear him". And that is my position. Some people don't like that – they don't like the way I speak publicly about matters that relate to God's word and the promises of God and, yes, it was because of that I was shot with three bullets a little while ago. But I'm not afraid. He took all fear from my heart and I keep going. I know people don't like me and they don't like what I say. But that's it. I live a day at a time. I thank God I'm still alive.'

I wondered whether living on the edge like this made him feel bitter towards those who were making his life difficult?

'No. We cannot live for the Lord, we cannot serve him, we cannot expect blessing from him, we cannot see growth, we cannot see the fullness of the Holy Spirit, if we have any grudges or bitterness in our hearts. That's true for any believer. If you want God to use you, you have to give up everything and look only to him.'

Finally, I asked Naim what he would like to say to the Christians in the west about their attitude to the word of God, Israel and the future of the church.

'I think they need to wake up. Pastors need really to go deeper into the word of God. They must not teach a "shadow" teaching. They must go deeper into the word of God and tell people the whole truth about what's in it. If a pastor does not know the fullness of God and the fullness of the word of God, how can he be a blessing to others and how can people really understand what's in the word of God? They need to open their hearts to understand that anybody who is anti-Israel and anti the Jewish people is really being anti-God and anti his word and his purposes.

'And Christians in the Holy Land need the Christians in the west to understand their position and they need your help and support. We are living in a very difficult situation. That's why we must join our hearts and hands and thoughts and minds and focus on the Lord of lords and King of kings, the Lord Jesus Christ.'

Chapter Eight

Shmuel Aweida
An Arab pastor of a Messianic Jewish congregation in Haifa

This story is so incredible, that's why it's unique . . . at the moment. But I suspect that before long we will hear of more peo-ple like Shmuel Aweida, as this trend of Arab Christians being reconciled to the people and nation of Israel continues to grow.

When Shmuel Aweida tells his story, he doesn't seem to find it all that surprising . . . perhaps because he is so ideally suited for what he's doing; his whole life has been a preparation for his work today. There can be no doubt that his parents' attitude to Jewish people and their Christian faith and understanding of the Bible had a profound effect on the young Shmuel. From the day he was born he was immersed in Jewish life and culture to the extent that he and his brothers naturally spoke Hebrew to each other at home. Born in 1968, Shmuel represents perhaps the first of a new generation of young Arab pastors in Israel who have grown up in a climate of reconciliation between Jew and Gentile and, despite recent and ongoing hostilities, are sure of what they believe, have a deep understanding of both Old and New Testaments, and a vision of what God is doing at this time that propels them forward.

Shmuel is under no illusions as to the spiritual battle that is being fought out for the soul of the nation of Israel. As you will read, he sees how far the country has moved from its biblical roots to embracing New Age philosophy and secularism; but despite this he believes, as an Arab, he is called to stand up for the God of Israel in Israel in order to bring the Jewish people back to their Messiah.

I am an Israeli Arab. I was born and grew up in Haifa. My parents were born in Israel, in a village close to Nablus. They were both believers. I have two younger brothers and we all attended Hebrew speaking Jewish schools. Although Arabic is our mother tongue, Hebrew is our main language and the language we use to speak to each other!

People ask me if I have a problem with my identity! Well you can't live in Israel and not be aware of the conflict between Arab and Jew. As a small child I can remember the Yom Kippur war of 1973, and a few years later when I was a teenager, I remember the war in Lebanon. But I grew up in a believing home and my identity as a believer has always been the strongest part of who I am. Believing the Scriptures and what God says about Israel before what people say about Israel has been the greatest influence on my life. Whilst growing up, 95 per cent of my friends were Jewish. Hebrew was my language. Therefore, compared to many, my upbringing means that I'm far from being a 'typical' Arab.

Today I am the pastor of the congregation in Haifa that I grew up in, Beit Eliahu, which means 'Elijah's House'. It's a Messianic congregation that's predominantly Jewish and reaches out to the Jewish people. People tell me that I must be a unique person in Israel, being an Arab pastoring a Jewish congregation; that may be true – I certainly don't know any other Arab pastors who are leading a Messianic congregation. However, the way I see it I'm a Gentile pastoring a Messianic congregation; the Bible doesn't differentiate between Arab, British or American . . . we're all Gentiles! It's Gentiles and Jews in God's sight! So maybe if I was an Englishman coming to pastor a Messianic congregation, that would be more sensational than an Israeli Arab who speaks Hebrew! Who knows?

At this point in the interview I felt Shmuel was reluctant to make a 'big deal' out of being an Arab in a predominantly Jewish situation because he didn't want to draw attention to himself in a way that would distract from the message he was seeking to share, so I asked him to describe how he was viewed by the local Jewish people he came into contact with on a daily basis . . .

Well, being a pastor of a congregation is not a position that is generally recognised in our Israeli society. If somebody asks me what I do and I reply that I'm the pastor of a congregation, they say, 'What's that?' Although the Messianic movement has grown significantly in recent years, there are still many people who have not met a believer face to face and talked to them about their faith in Yeshua. And so the questions start to flow, they become more and more interested and I usually end up sharing the gospel with them in a very natural way. The interesting thing is when they find out I'm an Arab; and I have to tell them I'm an Arab because I look Jewish and I sound Jewish. But, then when they realise I'm an Arab and they hear what I believe and how I feel towards Israel, they usually soften and shrug their shoulders and look puzzled and say it's weird enough that such a thing as a Messianic congregation exists, but being an Arab who pastors it is, well, interesting to them!

There have been times when I wished I was Jewish; times when I've shared the gospel with a Jewish person and they've turned round to me and said, 'This Yeshua is for you Arabs, he's not for us, why are you telling me this?' Other times I'm mistaken for a Jewish person and the response has been hostile; they've accused me of being a traitor and betraying the Jewish people by believing that Yeshua is the Messiah. Then I tell them I'm not Jewish, I'm an Arab and they stop to listen some more . . . to an Arab who loves Israel . . . 'How can this be?' they say to me. Then we go through God's plan of salvation . . . why did he choose Israel? And sometimes coming from an Arab makes them listen!

When I meet Christians from the west who believe in Replacement Theology I find it surprising that they can hold to such a position, because if people believe that God has rejected Israel – that they're not his chosen people any more – then how can they trust the rest of his promises? I've had my arguments with such people. On the other hand, I've also met people who are crazy about Israel . . . they'll do anything for Israel – except share the gospel. This is also a mystery to me! 'We'll give Israel anything we have but not Yeshua,' they say. I can't understand that attitude either. I believe such people support Israel blindly. I have no problem saying I'm pro-Israel, I support Israel. But when you know there are 60,000 abortions in Israel every year and the same people who love Israel fight abortion in England but don't care about the 60,000 who die yearly in Israel, it doesn't make sense to me. Or they pray against a gay parade in London, but turn a blind eye to the gay parades in Tel Aviv, Haifa and Jerusalem – it just doesn't make sense; it's as though they hold different standards. I can't see the apostle Paul being a member of such a church. I believe those two extreme views are both unbiblical.

God's standards remain the same. His salvation is the same for all. There is no other gospel except the one for the Jew first and then for us others.

I was very blessed to have the parents I had! They enabled me to grow up in Jewish surroundings and become familiar with Jewish traditions, and in one sense be part of Jewish life – not being a Jew but being part of Jewish life. Add to that the solid biblical teaching I received in the congregation, all this developed my understanding of life here and helped to make me the person I am today.

My father was fifty-five when I was born, and although he has died now, I remember him as being old and wise. He always told me that the Jews were God's people. Even before Israel became a state in 1948 there were immigrants coming to Israel both legally and illegally. During that time my father worked at the Haifa Municipality and he would help these Jewish immigrants to find jobs! He spoke Yiddish fluently. Our closest friends in the neighbourhood where we lived were holocaust survivors from Poland. So we grew up not just going to Jewish schools, but my parent's closest friends were Jewish too. In fact, in the neighbourhood where I grew up there were Jews and Arabs living in the same buildings. I realise that my experience is different to that of many other Arab families . . . but again, it has helped me to realise there is a better way than the hostility and division that we are confronted with so often today.

I know there are many Arab pastors who would not agree with me; I do not know them all personally. But I know some others who agree with my position. As for me, I will continue to teach the congregation that we are here for one reason – to glorify God and to make his name known in Haifa. Our congregation is called Beit Eliahu, House of Elijah, and just as Elijah confronted the prophets of Baal on Mount Carmel, and showed the people then who the only true God is; that's what I believe God is calling us to do – to confront the vast amount of idolatry here in Israel today. New Age philosophy is flourishing. Buddhism is flourishing. The mystical Jewish Kabala is also flourishing. All manner of other religions are attracting Israelis today. Each year many thousands of young Jewish people travel to places such as India and Thailand seeking a spiritual experience; as soon as they come out of the army they want to travel to clear their minds, and in the process they end up becoming involved with various Eastern religions.

At the present time we are putting together a team of young Jewish believers drawn from congregations all over the land to go to a big New Age festival that is staged near Tiberias during the Feast of Tabernacles in October. They will share the gospel with these spiritually hungry Israelis.

The biggest New Age festival in Israel is actually held during the Feast of Passover; thousands of people are worshipping idols in the form of these new religions instead of remembering how God brought them out of Egypt all those years ago. This demonstrates the spiritual hunger in Israel at the moment and the tremendous openness of the people to engage with other religions as they search for some spiritual reality. There are many such gatherings each year . . . some of them are extremely large, attracting twenty to fifty thousand people. And it's not just young people who are attracted to these events; families with young children also attend. Sometimes they are completely naked – attracted by free drugs, free sex . . . whatever. This is the Holy Land! The need for Yeshua is so strong. Jesus cried when he looked over Jerusalem; I think he would do the same today.

Today the Messianic congregations are growing . . . many are coming to faith in the Lord and this is very encouraging. But as I look to the future, I believe we will have to face some severe persecution, especially from the Orthodox Jews. Yesterday we were praying for one of the congregations in the south of the country that is facing much persecution from the Orthodox Jews there. I am anticipating that it will not be long before we face the same troubles here in Haifa.

I would like to ask the Christians in the west to understand what God is doing here today. Paul understood and taught that God has a plan for Israel (Romans 9—11). However, knowing what God is going to do eventually is one thing; in the meantime, what did Paul do? He went from place to place, starting at the synagogues, preaching the gospel. I know of no greater need in Israel today.

To pray for the peace of Jerusalem is to pray for the true peace that can only be found through the Prince of peace. The One New Man in the Messiah is a reality!

ISRAEL: THE MYSTERY OF PEACE

Julia Fisher

Israel: The Mystery of Peace contains incredible up-to-date true stories of hope and reconciliation from the Middle East that, rremarkably, are holding firm despite the ongoing unrest in Israel today. These stories, researched in depth by Julia Fisher, demonstrate that there is another road map for peace emerging in Israel today – God's road map – where, despite politics and war, Jews, Arabs and Christians are praying and working together demonstrating that genuine peace is possible.

Read about . . .

. . . **Jonathan Miles** who arranges for Palestinian Children from Gaza to have life-saving operations in Israel.

. . . **a nun from France** who walked across Europe to Jerusalem where she met a former Orthodox Jew, a German Protestant and an Arab Christian from the Old City . . . read how God has brought their paths together.

. . . **a couple from New York** who run an addiction centre for Arabs and Jews in northern Israel.

. . . **a man born** into a Muslim family in Algeria, who escaped from a terrorist training camp and is now living in Jerusalem, actively involved in reconciliation between Arabs and Jews.

. . . **R.T. Kendall**, the former minister of Westminster Chapel, who shares his experience of meeting and praying for Yasser Arafat.

LAND OF MANY NAMES
Steve Maltz

Much heat has been generated by the subject of Israel and Palestine. It's a subject that will not go away and it is crucial that Christians should have a clear grasp of both the spiritual and historical issues involved.

This is a lively, entertaining and provocative introduction to the subject for ordinary Christians. The author takes you on a historical journey of the *Land of Many Names*, from the Canaan of Abraham to the Promised Land, by way of the Land of Milk and Honey, Israel and Judah, Judea and Samaria, Palestine, The Holy Land, Zion, Israel and 'The Zionist Entity'. At each stage, we pause to consider what God is saying to all concerned and, in some places, awkward questions are also asked of the reader. This is an easy read, but it is not a comfortable book.

PEOPLE OF MANY NAMES
Steve Maltz

The Jews are a mystery to most, provoking a whole range of questions:

- Who are they?
- How have they survived for so long?
- Why have they been so feared or hated by so many people for so many reasons?
- What is their relevance to Christians?

This book attempts to give clear answers to these questions and helps the reader to understand the spiritual significance for both Christians and Jews.

This is a lively, entertaining and provocative introduction to the *People of Many Names*, from early beginnings in the Old Testament as the 'Children of Promise' and a 'Kingdom of Priests', then as the people of 'Galut' (Exile), where they were denigrated as 'Christ killers', 'Dhimmis' and 'Conspirators of Zion'. We view their accomplishments, despite the hostility that surrounded them, including the horrors of the Holocaust, and conclude our story in the New Testament, as the natural branches of God's olive tree.

HAS GOD FINISHED WITH ISRAEL?
Rob Richards

Much has been written and said by Christians on the whole issue of Israel, much of it triumphant, insensitive and simplistic. This book stems the flow. It is the journey of one man challenged, I believe, by God, to take a close look at the place of Israel within the purposes of God.

In this book, Rob Richards seeks to discover the answer to probing questions such as:

- Are Jewish people still the 'chosen people' and if so, for what?
- What does the Bible have to say about the covenants and the promised Messiah?
- How do events in Israel today fit in with biblical prophecy?